RON LEVINE

MICHAEL WOU

prisoners Of Age

The Alcatraz Exhibition

published by
synchronicity productions inc.,
5524 saint patrick street,
suite 333,
Montréal, québec,
canada H4E 1A8
www.prisonersofage.com

RON LEVINE - PHOTOGRAPHER
MICHAEL WOU - DESIGNER AND ILLUSTRATOR
FOREWORD BY ROBERT "ROSIE" ROWBOTHAM
INTRODUCTION BY DAVID WINCH
GERRY LIPNOWSKI - EDITOR

preface

In March 1996 I walked into a geriatric prison for the first time. I was expecting metal bars, tiny cells and hardened criminals ready to pounce from every dark crevice of the institution. What I found was not unlike a nursing home, but oddly juxtaposed with barbed wire and guard towers. There were men who required walkers, canes, wheelchairs... men attached to IV drips, oxygen tanks and catheters. My first thought was "what can these men possibly do to harm anyone on the outside while in this condition?"

It's hard to imagine these old men as criminals running from the law. You see the feebleness, the forgetfulness, the universal problems of senior citizens apparent in your own aging family members. And you tend to associate these fragile old men with men you've known. They could easily be our fathers or grandfathers. Ultimately, I couldn't help but be conflicted by these men and their stories: moved to pity by their frailty and a life squandered in prison, and simultaneously repelled by the crimes that necessitated their severe punishment—murder, rape, child molestation. And among their numbers, a generation of young people as well, a prelude to an aging prison population crisis to come.

Perhaps the most unexpected outcome of all was my own involvement in what started out as a simple photo shoot. That we would return to this prison three more times, and five others besides, never entered our minds during that first visit. The fact that our work culminated in this book and a number of exhibitions, including the first exhibit ever held at what is arguably the most infamous of prisons—Alcatraz—is in retrospect somewhere between a complete surprise and a total mystery. I'm not sure how we came to be on this path, but nevertheless, here we are.

First and foremost, this book is a photography book. It was never meant to be a treatise on the plight of the elderly in prison. We are neither journalists nor sociologists. We leave that work to the capable hands of those who spend their lives searching for answers in the criminal system.

However, we'd like to think that our exhibitions and book will raise awareness and initiate a public discussion on the issue of aging behind bars, and more importantly, shed further light on the need to prevent crime: to prevent the mistakes and ignorance, the hostility and hopelessness, that can condemn the young and often not-so-young to a lifetime imprisoned.

I hope you find these photographs compelling and worth examining. We present the stories of these most marginalized—and perhaps deservedly so—members of our society in their own words, which reveals much of themselves. What we as a society decide to do about them reveals just as much of ourselves ■

foreword
BY ROBERT "ROSIE" ROWBOTHAM

when I entered into the prison world, I was a young man in my early 20's. Reflecting back on those early days, I can clearly remember the stark and depressing prison setting. Most of us were young and anxious. Keen to get out and get back to our misadventures of choice. Egos were large, and tempers often short. However there was a sense of order and camaraderie. We took our lead from the older "cons" who spoke of respect, etiquette and principles, not decreed by our "keepers," but self-imposed within the ranks of the dismissed.

Hours were spent listening to the older convicts telling tales of prison life over the ages. Even the most cocky and tough prisoners would always defer to the aged. There was a civility and sense of respect for those who had spent much of their lives behind bars. There generally was something to be learned from the old-timers, or a laugh from an ancient joke passed on through the ages.

As over two decades passed, I grew older myself. My youthful spirit didn't disappear, but mellowed. I witnessed time pass and history unfold from a distance. I watched with sadness my family grow and move on. Within the prison walls, I also observed the whole prison dynamic change radically with the adoption of prison population integration: the mixing of prisoners incarcerated for all offenses, including sex offenders. Soon most prisons became inundated with a whole new prisoner component: multitudes of aging men.

Thousands of horror stories were uncovered in the 80's and 90's, resulting in the prosecution and incarceration of scores of abusive men, often survivors of the most horrific sexual assaults themselves. By default, we had to learn to live with these aging men. We lived in close quarters, but with clear divisions and boundaries.

Over time, all aged prisoners were questioned, often without any other basis than harsh prison generalizations. Many seniors were not sexual predators, but by-products of social dismissal. Older men incarcerated for crimes with roots involving acute poverty, addiction, illiteracy and marginalization. Men struggling to survive in a harsh, unrelenting materialistic world, were often landing in prison for long sentences in the twilight of their lives. Life was harsh for these elderly men in society, but even more so in the prison environment. The system was ill-prepared. Access for the disabled, special healthcare needs for the geriatric, dietary and medication needs generally were inadequate and the process for change painfully languid.

In 1996, while incarcerated, I was coldly informed of two personal tragedies which will never fade from my memory. My brother was murdered and my son was sexually assaulted. My rage, fueled by a very limited capacity to reach out and assist my grieving family members and child, tormented me to no end. The perpetrators in both nightmares were not brought to justice, and my personal circumstances catalyzed my pain. In a minimum security "camp," I was forced to interact with a myriad of aging sex offenders. I was forced to look at many around me with intense and macabre horror. I began to question. "How can they be torturing me in this environment?"

In the U.S., "three strikes you're out" legislation, drug laws like Michigan's "650 grams for life" and mandatory minimums have burgeoned prison populations. Corresponding with "brothers and sisters" housed in overcrowded and dismal gothic prisons has been heart-wrenching. Human beings receiving insanely long sentences with little or no hope for a future became commonplace. Rationality and logic dismissed for political gain at the expense of the lives of so, so many is far too often the norm. Why? There is no answer.

Now in the new millennium, in the height of technological advancement, never before have so many aged been incarcerated. Men who pose little or no threat to individuals or society. In the U.S. there are about 50,000 such men. In Canada, over 17 percent of the overall prison population are over 50 years old. Twenty-five to $60,000 annually is spent jailing these men with debatable, if any positive, outcome. Prison officials often agree it makes no sense. Still, with political agendas at the forefront, geriatric prison populations continue to grow.

RON LEVINE'S "Prisoners of Age" evokes haunting and intense emotions. He has masterfully captured the spirit of aged prisoners and engages all to learn and to question. Interviews bolster stories of woe which are shocking, occasionally pathetic, and encouraging pity and sympathy. A journalistic naiveness allows aging prisoners an unrestrained voice rarely, if ever, heard before.

RON LEVINE'S timing and skill is topnotch. He takes us on a journey of emotional introspection and pity. He explores issues and circumstances at a point when the floodgates are about to be overwhelmed. Will compassion prevail, or will our aged patriarchal prisoners fade from existence in cramped and decrepit surroundings? Revenge or reason? "Prisoners of Age" skillfully engages. You decide ∎

introduction
older inmates color prisons with shades of gray
BY DAVID WINCH

"my prison is becoming an old folks home"

WARDEN OF 3,000-PRISONER ANGOLA STATE PENITENTIARY IN LOUISIANA

"I was young and crazy," recalls ROLAND CAMPBELL, who is now aged 82. "I shot a woman; killed her. That put me in here. I had the devil in me... I wouldn't do nothing like that now."

The words of the elderly North Carolina prisoner are spoken with regret, but also with a rueful resilience. They sound off-key; old men and prison cells just don't mix. But in the United States and Canada today, they have to: elderly prisoners are a booming part of the prison population. From massive, hard-time southern prisons to campus-like low-security facilities in the North complete with geriatric wards, old cons are proliferating.

Old men behind bars don't generate any of prison's violent glamor, in contrast with convict icons played by PAUL NEWMAN, EDWARD G. ROBINSON or JAMES CAGNEY—who relentlessly scheme spectacular stunts to get out of Sing Sing, Alcatraz or southern chain gangs and to get back to real life. Nor are they usually the angry men who clang cups on their bars, raising hell and seething with resentment and violence.

Older prisoners are, on average, more like ROLAND CAMPBELL—reflective, quiet, with all the big events in their lives safely in the past. The McCain Correctional Hospital, a geriatric prison in rural North Carolina, is full of ROLAND CAMPBELLS. And soon, much of our prison systems will be, too. Seniors are quietly invading North American prisons in wheelchairs and on crutches, wearing white smocks and tied to their IV drips.

The new geriatric prisons they live in are different, too. They should be—these prisoners do not fit the crime-novel cliché of raw-edged young toughs pacing their cells like caged tigers, counting out the days and the years until their release, impatiently killing time till they can get out on the street again.

Old cons are more like toothless tigers: declawed, dazed, sometimes pathetic. But they can show sparks of the old spirit, like the somehow irrepressible inmates who escaped from one Alabama prison, and got as far as their legs would carry them. Then they gave in to physical exhaustion—two blocks from their cells. "They called me from the local hospital, and said, 'we got some of your boys,'" recalled the warden. "They done run out of breath."

. . .

Men in their 60's, 70's and 80's who are imprisoned—often hospitalized, really evoke sympathy, even pity, in a way younger prisoners just can't. They also bring a whole new range of complaints and grievances to bear, like the McCain convict whose appeal is based on his inability to wear his hearing aid in court: "I couldn't make out a word," he protests, recalling his bizarrely soundless trial.

Harsher penalties aside, a jarring fact is that many old cons are in prison today for crimes they committed when they were already in their late 50's, 60's, and even 70's: sexual abuse, assault, fraud, vehicular homicide, major property crimes, 1st degree murder. while some senior inmates are veteran convicts with a string of sentences stretching back to their teens and 20's, others are old men who were first convicted of serious crimes when they were already past retirement age. JONATHAN TURLEY, a washington D.C. law professor who deals with older prisoners, calls these offenders the late bloomers and overachievers of the criminal class.

In canada, where several seniors-oriented facilities have sprung up, one federal study confirms that, far from being simply the victims of longer sentences, 50 percent of older prisoners are first-time offenders. These convictions are, moreover, overwhelmingly for violent and sex-related offences. while quiet, elder prisoners usually have a calming effect on the general prisoner population, they are also subject to temper and emotional outbursts that can lead to crimes of passion: loss of inhibitions result in aggression, quarrelsomeness, rigidity and illegal sexual behavior, such as exhibitionism, concluded the canadian report. The authors speculate, quoting recent medical research, that changes in brain chemistry may result in a loss of inhibitions in some people as they age. This can lead to unexpected rages that prompt a law-abiding adult to suddenly commit a first crime even as they approach or pass retirement age.

This wave of older prisoners has begun to overwhelm traditional facilities like the Angola state maximum security facility in Louisiana where in 1995, for the first time, more inmates died than were paroled. To cope with the change, a new generation of specialized prisons has grown up, as far afield as Oregon, pennsylvania, Alabama, North carolina and ontario. one of the most prominent is in Hamilton, Alabama.

with the grandfatherly air of a weekend putterer, THURMON JETTON shows off
his garden to visitors. bright floral colors shoot up in every direction as marigolds,
petunias, old maids and zinnias all blossom in the scorching alabama sun. JETTON,
dressed in a white work outfit, leans back on his heels and strikes a backpockets-
casual pose, while his ragged grey eyebrows and lively eyes give him a sheepish,
somewhat mischievous look. in his smoky southern drawl, JETTON describes his
handiwork with obvious pride.

The affable gardener's floral tapestry hardly suggests the hand of a murderer.
but at age 68, THURMON JETTON is in his 16th year in prison and, as he readily recounts,
in a tone as lively as the one he uses to talk about his garden, he earned his sentence.

"well," he recalls, matter-of-factly, "i took up with a man's wife," and in a
chain of events as predictable as a country music song, her husband soon found out
and she fluttered back to him. JETTON, "bad drunk," grew enraged. "me and him got
to arguing. i brought out the ball bat. she's lying on the bed, and i grab the ball bat
to kill him—no use denying that—i'm goin' to kill him. just as i swing at him, she run
out between me and him and i caught her right there," he concludes, pointing to his
forehead: "killed her deader than a doornail."

NOW THURMON JETTON faces old age in prison, an existence marked out by
parole hearings leading like highway signs to a territory on the edge of life and death,
freedom and despair. so while the local wal-mart in hamilton, alabama, sprawls
invitingly just beyond his garden fence, JETTON will never be able to amble over to
pick up a hoe or some fertilizer. if he did, his every move would be followed through
the sights of a smith & wesson 10-gauge shotgun trained on him from a nearby
watchtower. an infinite distance separates him from a normal retirement.

• • •

JETTON is not alone in this predicament: while the average age of convicts in U.S. federal facilities is just 37, reports the federal Bureau of prisons, there were 50,000 prisoners aged over 50 in the mid-1990's, out of about one million inmates. That total has continued to grow as a steady five to seven percent of the inmate population. Some projections foresee more than 125,000 older prisoners in the early 2000's, as the U.S. prisoner population surges toward two million. Similarly, in Canada, despite a drastically smaller prison population, the trend is obvious: a recent report by the federal correctional service noted that the rise of older prison inmates nationally in the mid-1990's was almost 10 times that of younger offenders.

In the U.S., the effect of longer sentences and three-strikes laws, which mandate life sentences for third offences, will almost certainly keep this number growing. These laws deny judges and juries the right to fix sentences that are elastic—depending on a prisoner's behavior and prison conditions. Instead, they impose mandatory life sentences on third convictions. This can mean that a 45-year-old murderer or rapist will almost certainly spent his next 30-plus years in prison, with no possibility of release. If it is his third conviction, even lesser crimes will carry this life sentence. And since the number of convictions is increasing rapidly, the length of sentences may lead to an elephant-in-the-boa phenomenon of a large wave pushing through the system. This could hugely inflate the number of older prisoners.

The costs of this crime-fighting approach are, by all accounts, very high. An average inmate costs taxpayers in the U.S. $20,000 a year to keep in prison. Meanwhile, a geriatric prisoner, with all the complex medical facilities and personal care that become necessary, costs closer to $60,000 a year.

What is that buying? For this growing minority of seniors, old age is not about long walks, waiting patiently for the mail and pension check to come, much less rounds of golf in Florida or Arizona. Instead, it revolves around iron bars, annual pleas to the parole board and endless cellblock hours in prison whites like those JETTON wears, loudly stencilled in black: "Department of corrections."

Hamilton is a small, plain-looking town in northwest Alabama, with a small suburban strip of McDonald's and shopping malls at the town's edge. It seems an odd spot for one of the pioneering U.S. prison facilities for seniors. The full name is the Hamilton Institute for the Aged and Infirm, or Hamilton A+I, but inmates scornfully refer to it as Hamilton Lay and Die, for its odd mix of nursing home dreariness and barbed-wire limits. A low-rise former mental-health facility, Hamilton A+I is ringed by high fences that most prisoners could not hope to climb, and ominous-looking guard towers.

Physically and psychologically, only this barrier separates the Hamilton prison from the Sunset Home nursing residence across the street. The facility was designed to house prisoners who are older or who require more medical attention. Today, Hamilton A+I's inmate population of 255 also includes many younger inmates, some in their early 20's—they do the hospital lifting, maintenance and kitchen work— as well as handicapped and soon-to-be-released prisoners. Inside Hamilton, the traditional prison culture of tattoos and tough guys mixes uneasily with a geriatric-oriented nursing wing filled with IV drips and bedridden inmates. For first lunch call at 11 a.m., a ragged queue studded with wheelchairs, walkers, crutches and canes crowds together near the dining hall, evoking not so much a hard-knocks southern prison as it does the waiting room at Lourdes.

Like virtually every prison in the U.S., its population offers a cross-section of working-class males. Plenty of truck drivers and longshoremen, day laborers and farm workers, men whom the census likes to describe as "unskilled."

A busy nursing station straddles the heart of the facility ("INMATES ARE NOT TO KNOCK ON OR LOOK IN THIS DOOR") to care for elderly prisoners such as LEON DAVIS, a wheelchair-bound 69-year-old. DAVIS was already handicapped in 1987—he suffered the amputation of both feet following diabetes in 1979—when he unloaded a .357 Magnum at his girlfriend. With surgical precision, he describes the four shots ("one near the heart, two in the stomach and one in the groin") that he fired after an explosive series of disputes with her. She survived. DAVIS got 25 years for attempted murder. Reflecting on their fates, DAVIS concludes, "she got disability, I got time."

...

A charming and affable black man with a deep rum Alabama accent, DAVIS praises the medical attention he receives at Hamilton. "It's easier in a wheelchair here" than in the hard-time maximum security prisons he had been in previously, says DAVIS. There, older prisoners are routinely victimized by younger ones. Still, he still finds Hamilton's mix of old and young prisoners, mentally unstable and low-risk inmates a bit unsettling.

"They bring crazy folks in," complains DAVIS, adding, "when I see a fella, if he talks crazy, I don't have nothin' to do with him. But the young fellas, I'm glad they're here. Don't none of 'em give me no problems." On a philosophical note, DAVIS reflects on the dilemma of old men in prison: "At 65 or 70, a man's life is just about over with. It's hard to stay here without gettin' mixed up. I got to look up my family; don't know where 'bout half of them is. I'm not coming back to prison; I'm too old. I'm just tryin' to get straight with GOD."

We make an emotional trade-off with young prisoners: they may be locked into a rough situation but, hey, they deserved it. Convicts may have had bad childhoods, rough lives, a hard-knocks upbringing, but we cannot let ourselves think about that: we have to protect ourselves. Better for them to be in there than out here threatening our children, we conclude. We fear them and want to punish them, and above all to control and restrain them. They may be underdogs, but they are dangerous underdogs. They personify a looming menace, the physical threat of strong young men. Apprehension, anxiety, flat-out fear—these reactions are often at the core of our attitudes toward lawbreakers in their 20's and 30's.

With old men behind bars, it's different. Despair, sorrow and bitterness predominate. Older prisoners evoke a new spectrum of emotions: pity, bathos, and even a sense of the comic futility of some of misadventures that landed them in prison at—what!?!—62 years of age.

older prisoners, then, are neither fish nor fowl: they occupy a gray area. Their situation is usually no longer obviously threatening, but they remain behind bars. They are often the victims of fierce persecution and picking-on by younger prisoners. As a result, the new institutions that are being designed to house them are more like nursing homes than prisons. Medical care and medium-to-low security environments replace the walls of traditional penitentiaries.

Hamilton warden W.C. BERRY, a burly tobacco-chewing Alabaman with a poster of his beloved Crimson Tide college football dynasty dominating the office wall, speaks slowly but firmly about the predicament of old men in prison. "Protecting society is the key role of prisons," says BERRY, a likable man whose skepticism about rehabilitation leads him to argue that many old convicts are not going to change. While they may look pathetic behind bars in wheelchairs and the incarceration of a seniors' prison can seem excessive, BERRY underlines cases in which murders or sexual abuses were committed by handicapped or gravely ill seniors. He warns against the natural impulse to treat decrepit-looking older prisoners as if they were incapable of harming anyone. "The recidivism rate is huge," stresses BERRY, "particularly for sex offenses."

BERRY realizes, moreover, that a well-adapted prison like Hamilton is far better than an offender will find elsewhere. His files bulge with letters from senior prisoners at traditional, tougher state facilities, often virtually begging to be transferred to Hamilton, where they hope that they will not be victimized by gangs of younger convicts.

Given their senescence, do older, sick or bedridden inmates belong in prison? As one 65-year-old at McCain Correctional Institute asks, wearily: "How do I go about getting a time cut?" Is there really a need to protect society with iron bars from a convict like OTIS WYATT?

· · ·

WYATT, 84, is one of the deans of prisoners at Hamilton A+I. The wheelchair-bound inmate has a slight shock of wild gray hair, bracketed by white eyebrows and protruding ears. Much of his time is spent in the main prison common area, hunched over, reading, while other prisoners languidly watch TV. In the last months of his conviction for sexually molesting a girl ("I DIDN'T DO IT"), WYATT is preparing for release, hopefully before he is 85. With the end of the tunnel in view, WYATT freely blasts prison life: "Damned right I'll be glad to get out of here."

Looking to life beyond the bars, the cantankerous WYATT offers his views straight-up. He doesn't like the blend of young and old at Hamilton: "You got all kinds mixed up; I got nothing to do with the young ones." He slams the medical service for neglecting the chronic pain in his leg: "They don't give you nothin' more than Tylenol… You'd be dead before the doctor would see you." As for the guards, WYATT is bracing: "They're strict, even on the old guys. The officers are hell on you. They're always trying to get you to take a bath!" In a conspiratorial tone, as if informing a human-rights monitor, he confides, "And even if you've had a bath, they make you take a second one!"

The American Civil Liberties Union, prison reformers and critical criminologists—decried by some conservatives as the penological left-wing—argue that prisoners like OTIS WYATT should be treated in hospital-like wards. There, they would be much freer to come and go. It is far less expensive, and a much better use of detention space at a time when convictions are soaring, to release prisoners when they pass the criminal 'menopause' age that criminologists have tried to define.

The Sentencing Project, a prisoner advocacy and justice group, points out that 66 percent of people arrested are under age 30. It concludes that since crime rates for most offenses drop sharply after age 30, three strikes and you're out (LAWS) "will result in imprisoning a group of offenders for life who might be more appropriately sentenced to shorter terms of imprisonment until they age out of criminal activity." The ACLU emphasizes that only one percent of all serious crimes are committed by people over age 60.

Reasonable people may wonder: what threat is posed by a doddering old man like JAMES BLALOCK, currently housed in the MCCAIN INSTITUTE?

After recounting a long and complicated story involving drug-dealing, a 20-year sentence and police seizing $10,000 cash, his seiko watches and personal possessions, the 66-year-old BLALOCK gets to the heart of his plight: HOW does he get out?

"HOW can I go about getting a clemency act, because, as you can see, I'm eat up with emphysema, I'm on three sprays a day, and a pill three times a day. That's just for respiratory breathing. I've got a shoulder here that they've squirted cortisone in twice, which hasn't helped—at times, I can't even raise my left arm. I'm just all messed up."

"NOW, how do I go about getting some help on my sentence?" Experience and sentencing laws suggest very little can be done.

And what will become of the similarly ailing JAMES VEACH?

VEACH, 88, walks with a cane and appears hale, but the tall, white-haired senior is quite deaf, and a conversation requires many high-decibel exchanges ("HOW LONG... IS YOUR SEN-TENCE?"—"EH?"). VEACH can still protest lucidly about the incident that led to his sentence on murder charges in 1996. In a dispute over an 18-inch stretch of his land overlapped by a neighbor's fence, he pulled out a shotgun and blasted his neighbor four times. The wounded man staggered back to his home, where he died. VEACH retorted in court that the neighbor had attacked him with a hoe, and he reacted in self-defense. He will serve his murder conviction in HAMILTON A+I for a decade, remaining outwardly impassive over his fate, awaiting parole in 2006 when he will be... 94.

Victim-rights groups argue that the age of an attacker is irrelevant: if someone is guilty of assault or rape, they should do the time sentenced, even if that leads to old men being jailed in perpetuity. Protecting society from frail old men, however, may turn out like destroying the village to save it, if the prison population keeps surging upwards at great cost to the public sector.

• • •

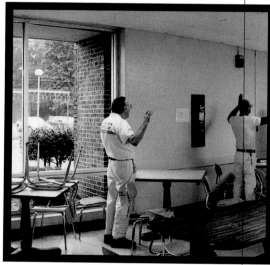

At the Warkworth Institution in Ontario, Canada, inmate HELMUT BUXBAUM, 60, proposes that the federal Young Offenders Act, which sets the ground rules for juvenile justice, be matched with an older offenders act. This would recognize the distinct physical and mental health needs of senior prisoners. It might, for example, reward prisoners' good behavior with early transfer to ward-like, low-security prison hospitals where visits from family would be much less difficult and stressful. Or require community service for the right to return to civil society where they could "undemonize" themselves.

But the prospects for geriatric prisons and new possibilities of early parole for disabled convicts all fade into the horizon of speculation and wishful thinking for an aging old convict like WALKER SMITH. Still, he manages to express nothing but sunny sentiments.

A slim, fragile-looking 76-year-old with a sharply protruding lower lip, SMITH was convicted on a murder charge in 1983 in Lee County, Alabama. He had killed his mother in a rage by repeatedly stabbing her with a kitchen knife in a dispute over whether she would wash his laundry.

SMITH was first sent to Alabama's rough Kilby Prison, before being transferred to Hamilton A+I. "It's the best place I've been in. There are maybe two, three guys who give you trouble, that's all." SMITH, who suffers recurrent health problems, praises the prison health facilities: "Since I slipped bad on the bathroom floor, I've never been in as good shape. But you get good attention here; it's closed in and convenient." As for his prospects, scarcely a wisp of despair clouds SMITH's horizons. "I've been before the (PAROLE) board twice. They turned me down; said I was not ready. I go back in May."

As he strikes a match to his lumpy, hand-rolled cigarette, SMITH emphasizes his hopes. "I believe in the Ten Commandments, in JESUS CHRIST, in prayer," he says, smiling. "All I can say is, thank GOD for bringing me this far."

Before SMITH can finish a drag on his cigarette, he is drowned out by the evening chapel meeting in the nearby canteen, where inmates suddenly raise their voices in a wobbly verse of Amazing Grace.

"Through many dangers, toils and snares,
    I have already come.
    'Tis Grace hath brought me safe thus far,
    And Grace will lead me home."

But for the WALKER SMITHS of this world, it may well take more than grace to lead them home ∎

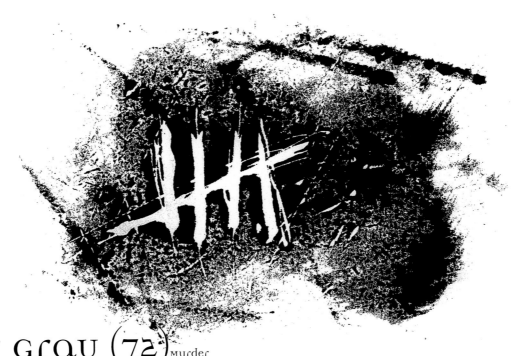

elliot gray (72) murder

never been in prison before. I was retired and
lived with my daughter. I was given three years.
this leg has been off for 15 years and I was getting
disability. I used to work on a pipe line. I was
a heavy duty operator. I've been in Hamilton
(prison) about a month. they said that I molested
a young girl. but I didn't do it. I've got arthritis
in my shoulder. this leg pains and it's getting
worse. you might be dead before a doctor would
see you. you've got to have an appointment for
everything. you can't tell when it is going to hit
you, but it is about once a month and lasts 19
hours. you can't sleep with the hurt. these
officers are mean. they wake you up. they are
sure strict. they always want you to take a bath.
I have to take two a day sometimes ∎

otis wyatt
sex crime (84)

ABOVE (55) bobby miller. sex crime
RIGHT (72) carl reynolds. habitual drunkeness
FAR RIGHT (47) ervin jessie. sex crime

sanscot

(72)

TOMMY (63) stone
sex crime

This state has the habitual offenders act and if you got three or more priors, they can give you life without. I met three guys at west Jefferson (PRISON) when I was going through barber school. All three of them was from Mobile county (ALABAMA), same place I was from. All three of them had life without. You know what they got life without for? one stole four hubcaps, one stole eight cartons of cigarettes, and one stole a bicycle. Up where you're from, they'd throw it out of court. They wouldn't even hear it. Not Alabama! ∎

(66) trafficking
james blalock

How can I go about getting a time cut or getting a clemency act 'cause, as you can see, I'm eat up with emphysema, I'm on three sprays a day, and a pill three times a day. That's for just respiratory breathing. I've got that wrong with me, I've got a shoulder here that they've squirted cortisone in me twice, which it hasn't helped, at times I can't even raise my left arm ■

"I'm just all messed up."

(58)
"Honest AMOS"

I've been in and out of prison pretty much all my life. I was abandoned when I was six months old, I was in an orphanage since I was eight, I was in reform school from 12-15 and graduated to prison at 15 and been in prison ever since. ...

murder (64) JIM elder

Has a son, five grandchildren, and is married to his second wife for the past 10 years. They met in prison, in christian fellowship after being introduced by a minister/friend at p4w.

when I first came into the prison system, years ago, the type of inmate back then were career criminals, and there was some element of respect, of doing time back in those days. you didn't hear tell of sex offenders and pc inmates... there was none of that sort of thing. There was kind of a stand-up policy in the institution. you were your own man. you acted like a man. you were treated as a man. And today's criminal, well I shouldn't call him a criminal, they're just misfits of civilization as we know it. Drug addicts, AIDS victims, they're not career criminals, they're just misfortunate people of the world. And I just find it hard to do time with these kind of people today. They scare you in a way because they have no ethics about life. They've got no social education, they don't know how to interact, they're sleazy. They're not what you'd call a very good element of inmates.

when I started doing time, the career criminals who were in the institution were bank robbers, two-story men, cat men, funny money, safe guys, swag guys... you don't see these people anymore. They're all into drugs now. It's sad. It's not getting any better, it's actually getting worse. A majority of the younger set that have been coming in, they're addicts. The government has closed down a number of the facilities, for tax cuts or whatever reason. Now they go to street drugs and get themselves in jackpots, they get into heroin or crack, and starts to stealing and they end up in the prison system. And they're happy to be here. I was talking to this young guy, 23 years old, who tells me "jim, when I'm out, I'm lonely." I says, "geez, you're 23 years old. what'd'ya mean, you're lonely? you've gotta be kidding, guy. There's a whole world out there. Did you ever think about going to other countries? Different cultures." "No," he said.

"The old guys had a code.
These guys don't have any code."

I'm what they probably consider one of the most high profile guys across the board. I'm one of the guys that started prisoner justice day in canada. My crew at that time, we changed the system as to prisoners' rights and what they have today. The grievance system, the TVs and radios, the things they have in their cells today are the things that we fought for. A lot of them died to change the system. And I often say today, it's a shame, because if the guys that are dead could see what it's turned to be, they would roll over in their graves. It's almost a shame to see how we'd changed the system, 'cause actually the system prior to that was a fair system. And now you're dealing with the people that you're dealing with today, these type of inmates.

Authorities consider me a danger. These people have screwed me so much over the years. And they know I'm just blowing up with hate for the system because of what they've done to me. They've beat me. I've seen them murder inmates. out and out murder them and get away with it. so I know a lot about the system and how dirty it is. The system 30 years ago was nothing like the system today. The work projects they have, pilot projects, it's all a scam. It's a taxpayers rip-off. Here I am doing time because I broke the law, and I'm in a system that's more corrupt than anything I can possibly think of people doing on the street. They bring drugs into the institution and then they push policies against drug strategies. There's a bartering system that goes on. You pay $23 for a carton of cigarettes in the canteen. There's gambling and drug dealing. Dealing in cartons and so-on. Your staff may sell you 12 cartons of cigarettes for a $100, cash. Racketeering, that's the short term. They know it, they don't do anything about it.

All the old career criminals, you don't find them anymore. Us guys like myself, we're like dinosaurs. We're all dinosaurs of the old system. The old guys had a code. These guys don't have any code. Everything goes. There's no honor among them. They'll get in debt in drugs and they won't pay it, they'll go to the man, they'll rat on them. This is the kind of element. To an old timer like me, these kind of people have no value to me. They're garbage. And it's a shame that I'm doing life and that I have to be associated with that kind ∎

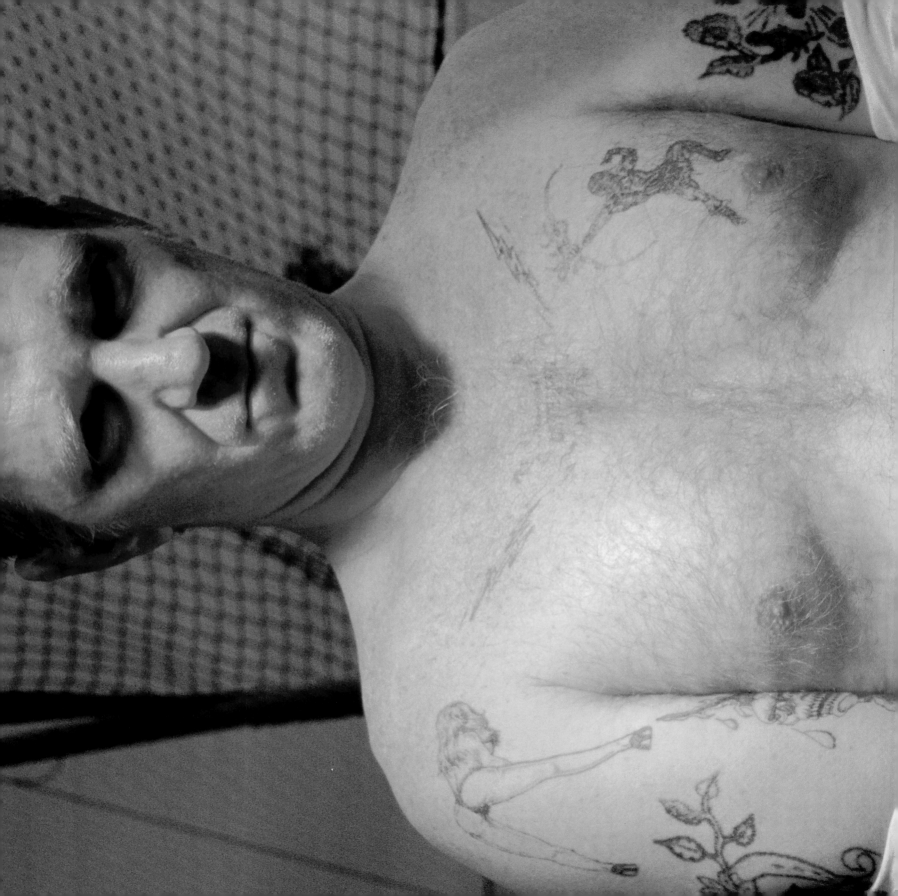

ricky "sheepdog" smith, serving (42) 198 years
robbery, burglary, escape.

calvin selman

murdered a convenience store couple because they didn't let him have credit on

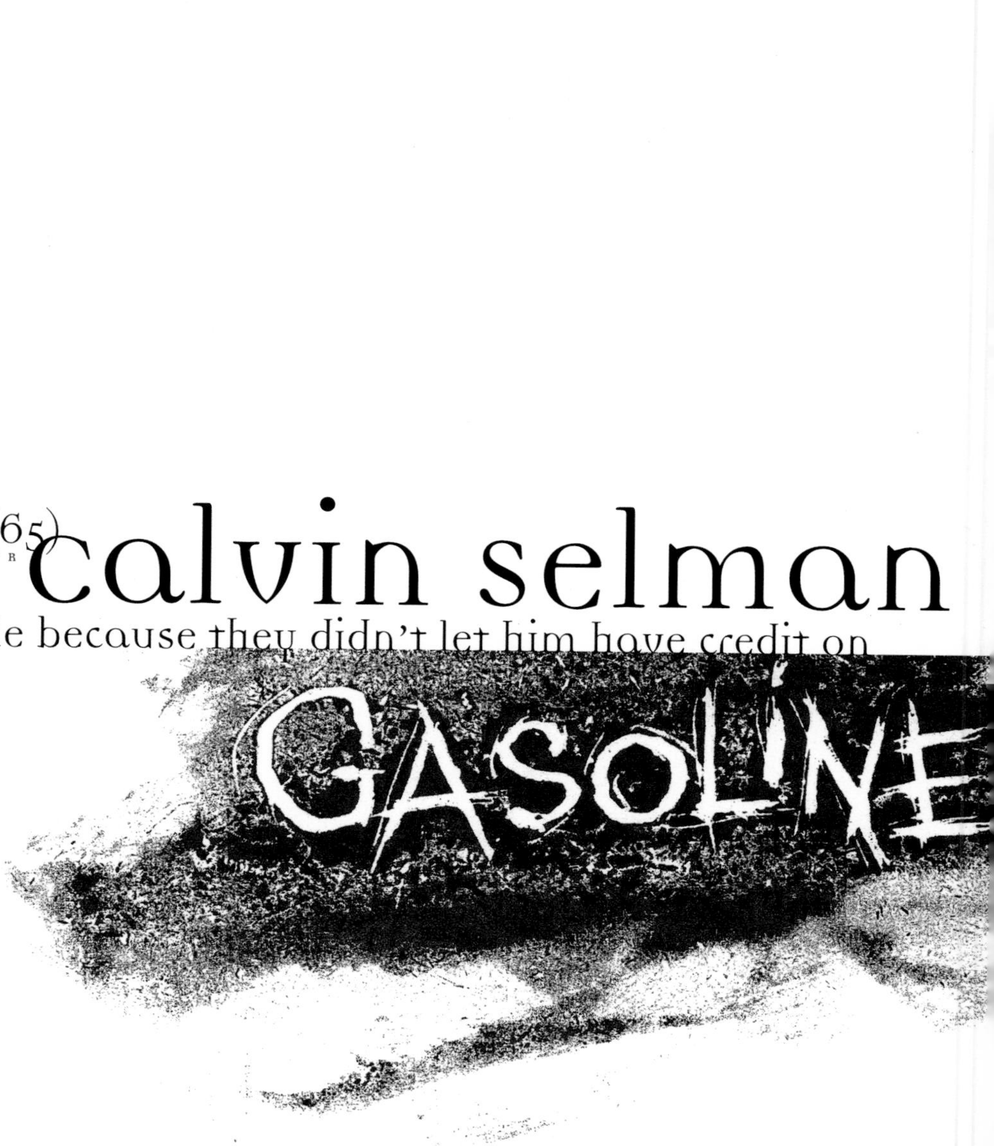

GASOLINE

I was in a one man lock up cell at HOLMAN (PRISON) ever since '69. All us lifetimers went to Holman when they tore old KILBY (PRISON) walls down. I wrote "HELLO DARLING" sittin' in a one man lock-up cell. Got it out to one of the correctional officers to get out to CONWAY TWITTY. He recorded it. Gave me $2,500 for it. I sold him the copyrights and everything ∎

arthur
forrester
(prison records incomplete)

they don't care what you do. the only thing they're interested is to keep you and keep you and keep you. I reckon it's because of the politicians or something. they got everybody locked up, they're going to keep them locked up. No matter what circumstance they've got now. there's a money situation in this. somebody's getting money off of someone here. they couldn't afford to keep housing people and warehousing people and just keep them locked up. they just keep putting them in and putting them in, and it's a cycle they've got to do something about because they're going to have a prison in every town, every city if they don't do something about it. they're wanting to build more (PRISONS) for everybody. they just keep on crowding y'all. getting you closer and closer together and they don't know why all the people fight. you take 1,400, 1,500 men and you're gonna have fights. you're gonna have arguments. No room to breathe or nothing like that. old guys fighting and everything. It's all over. Man, I've been seeing this since '86. I know what I'm talking about. you just gotta run. you just gotta run. and most of them, they don't wanna fight. some people just can't walk away. and I've been walking away. I've been spit on and everything else since I've been in here working my time. so I'm rehabilitated. so I can go back on the street. I wouldn't want to be around guns or nothing like that. alcohol or nothing like that. I wish they would ban it all ∎

5I)

ommf johnson $6 (8I)

felony for a $6 overdrawn check.

IT's not bad as far as the officers and the camp is concerned, but I've been here six months and I've seen a lot of people die. A lot. There's been 10 people dead since I've been here. Which they will probably crack my ass if they hear me say that, but they don't help nobody. I am trying to get away from here because there is a lot of hepatitis. There is one guy with hepatitis B and he is working in the kitchen. That is just fucked up man and I'm trying to get away from here before I get it. I came here healthy and I want to leave healthy. This place kind of drags you down a lot too. 'cause these old people, you kind of get close to them and they often die on you ■

jonathan (27) shadrick

ROBBERY

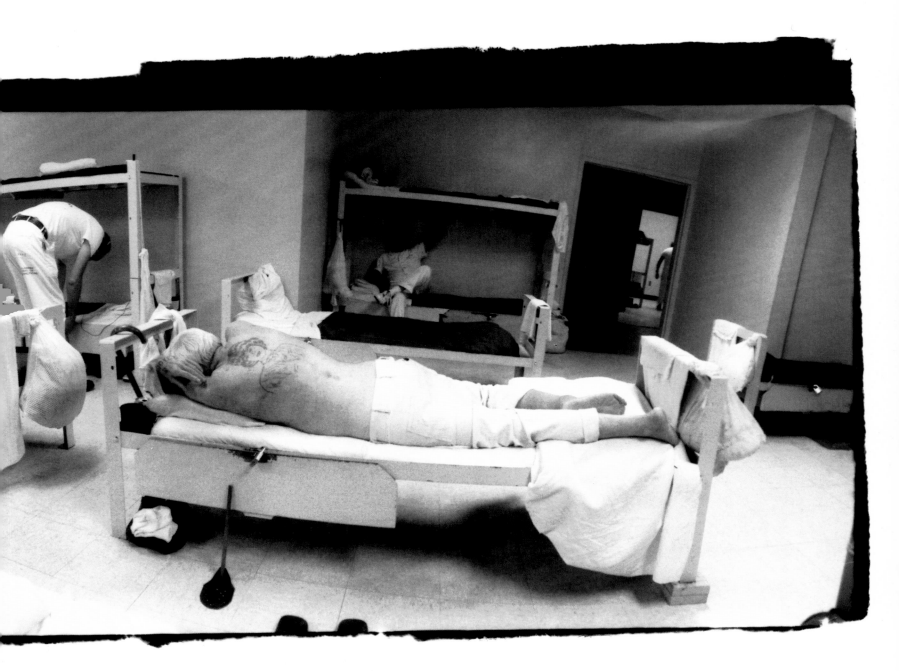

john (61)
(prison records incomplete)
ollison

charles DAVID stanley

(69) MURDER

I was convicted of killing my wife for harassing me. My trial lasted five days. Two days to pick a jury. Two days to find me guilty of 1st degree murder and one hour to give me the death sentence. I killed her for harassing me. For wanting more money that I did not have. She had me locked up three different times. On account that she wanted more money. I was giving her what money I could afford, because I was only on social security and disability. I was still keeping the house payments up and I had moved out and moved in with my sister. We was getting a divorce. And I gave her the home and everything else. And I says, "you can have it all, just let me go and be by myself." And she would not do this because she wanted more money. And I didn't have no more money to give her ∎

she got to accusing me that I was going with some other
girls, you know. And cussing at me, same thing she always
did. We would go to the supermarket and girls speak to me
and she would tell me, "Is that your girlfriend?" I tell you,
she got jealous and all, and you know how I feel about it.
If I had to do it all, I'd do it over again, I would ∎

Leo
(76) Eason

"I killed my wife in 1988." murder

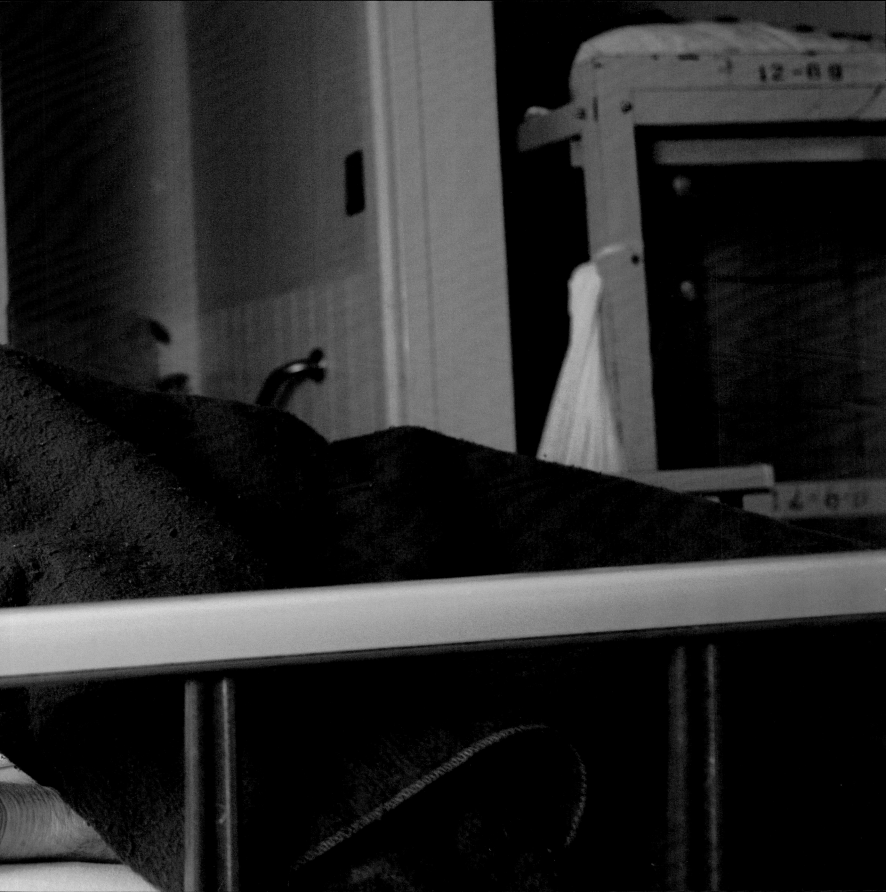

every state is needing more facilities like this. Alabama needs more right now.
we don't have the space that we need to provide this type of care for inmates.

The old men want peace and quiet. But the youngsters will look
for trouble and cause trouble and they're constantly picking at
them and causing problems. That's one reason this place is so
smooth back here. we got an aged population. it's laid back.

The majority of them were on drugs or drinking. And we've got a lot
of sex-offenders here. A lot of these old men, sex offenders, child
molesters, pedophile-types. we've got quite a few of those older
generation here like that. we've got one guy here who was molested
by his father years ago. And now he's here. And you hear the stories
about how they were molested while they were children—that's
why they act the way they do—there's a lot of truth in that. They
grow up, they're just like their father figure who molested them.

we try to find them a home plan. parole board will. quite often you'll find
that family members are not able to give them the kind of care we give
them. They end up staying in prison. if they don't have a suitable home
plan for parole, they will turn their parole down. Therefore they stay with
us. The parole board is not guaranteed to give them parole. And if it's not a
good home situation, the family can't care for them, they'll turn him down.

in 1984, a guy here got out and he had some mental problems; went
back to southern Alabama, stayed out five or six months, got caught in
a grocery store stealing a six-pack of beer and a t-bone steak and a loaf
of bread. He comes back. He's an A+I (AGED AND INFIRMED) inmate. I ask him,
"why did you get back in trouble?" "I was hungry and didn't have
anywhere to go." And he's an older guy. six months to a year later, he
died here. He was losing his mind here and there, but he knew he had
nowhere to go, he was hungry, he wanted a six pack of beer, a steak and
a loaf of bread and he went and got it. And of course, he got caught and
he got sentenced for it ■

Billy OWEN
(warden)

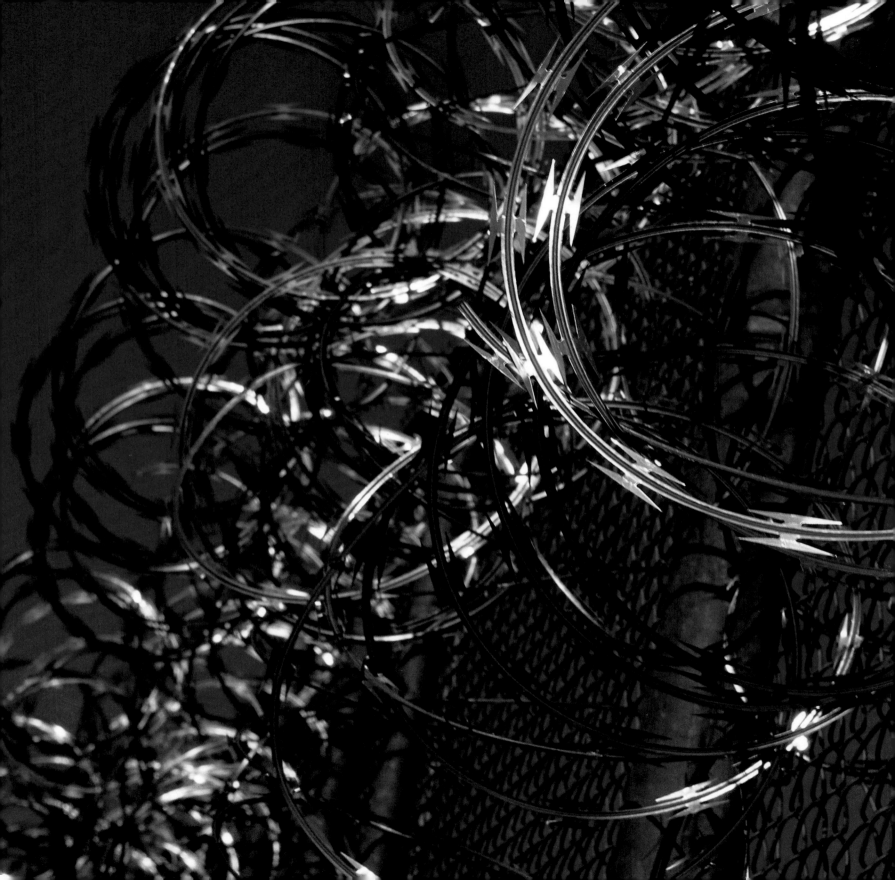

OFF LIMITS
UNAUTHORIZED
PERSONNEL
~WILL RECEIVE~
DISCIPLINARY ACTION
PER ORDERS, WARDEN

six bypass surgeries while in prison.

James B. Thorneberry

(66)

assault

He shot two men who were trying to rob him. "They were dressed up as boy scouts (WHEN THEY APPEARED IN COURT), turned the tables on me and they brought their girlfriends with them and the judge blamed me."

Spider)

Troy Borden (29) theft

"I'm a racist. A hard core racist on the streets too."

I'll hook back up with a supremacy group. It's my goal in life to see a whole civil war take over America. If it was left up to me, I would annihilate the race (BLACK) from the face of the earth. A lot of people man, they don't agree with me that I know Aryan Nation, Neo Nazi skin heads of America. All those people I used to run around and sell guns to because my belief that everything west of the Mississippi should be given back to the American Indians. West Texas, New Mexico, Arizona and about three quarters of California should be given back to Mexico because we stole that land. East of the Mississippi? That's our land dude ■

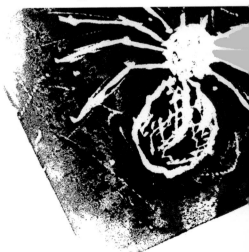

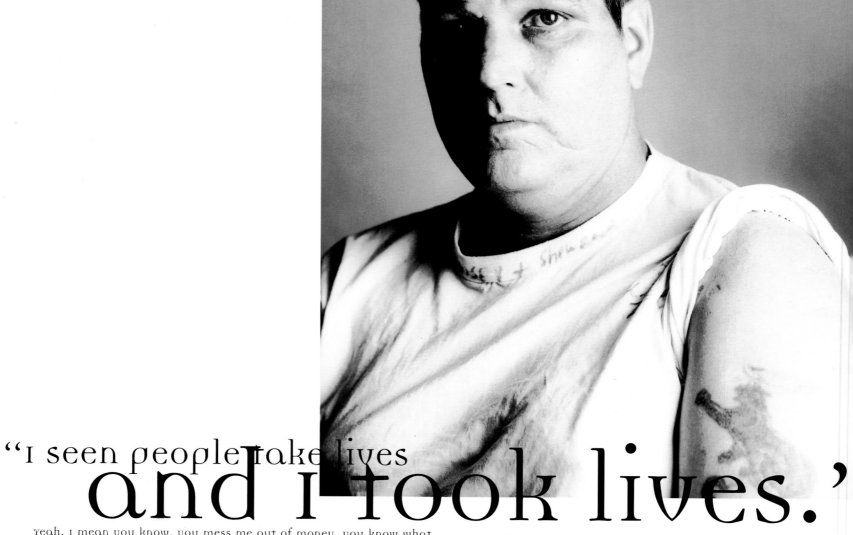

"I seen people take lives
and I took lives.'

yeah, I mean you know, you mess me out of money, you know what
I mean, and I find out that it's a lie, well you're dead. you wind up taking
what you want and them trying to take what you got. It's fight or die.

I lost my family, you know. Here when I was locked up. I lost my mother and my father, and
my brother got stabbed to death in Angola penitentiary. And my sister, she died by a blood clot.
I got sclerosis of the liver. I don't know how much time I have left. Hopefully it will be a while ■

Terry Moore (47)
Burglary, Robbery, possesion of stolen property

I had trouble with a police officer, in Utah. That's why I'm all the way here. He shot me. I shot him back. That's what put me in trouble. He didn't hurt me too bad. I didn't hurt him too bad. And then they gave me 10 years for that.

Things have changed since the time I come in. I've seen a lot of change, I have. It (prison) will make you come to be a better man. It will learn you a lesson, little things that I was quick to do when I was out—I will not be quick to do it. I know what things are like now. I really know myself now. I'm hanging in there ∎

john wilson
Attempted murder

(76)

(30) rowe

dwayne
Burglary

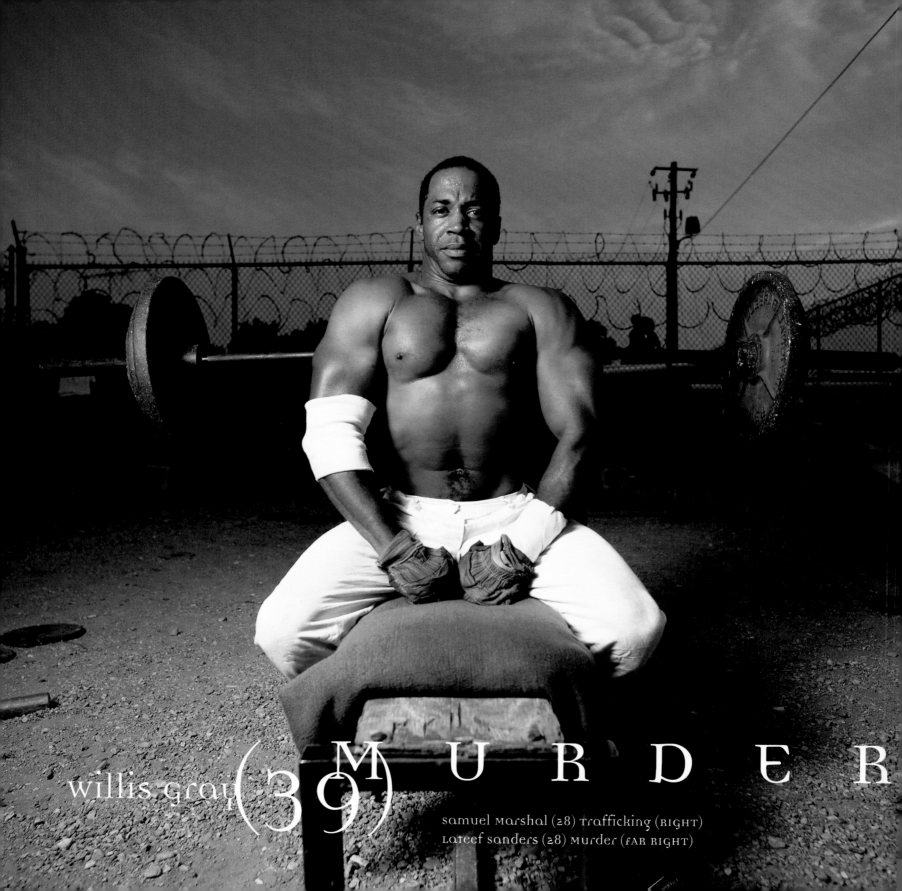

willis gray (39) MURDER

samuel marshal (28) trafficking (RIGHT)
lateef sanders (28) murder (FAR RIGHT)

(59)
james albert wright
given 40 years for running a gambling house.

"what I would like to do. I would like to write a book for young black people. Tell them that this ain't the way, this ain't the way. You don't do it this way."

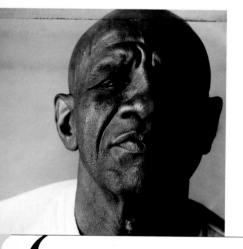

It was 1959, in Birmingham (ALABAMA). A lot was going down. We were struggling with the civil rights thing, and Dr. Martin Luther King was leading it. And I had come down there with this organization. Well, I got 50 years. Snatching $24 out of a man's hand. When they passed it, I didn't even think about it (THE RACIAL MOTIVE). 'Cause all I was thinking about is, I get the chance, I'm gonna escape, and I did. I've escaped three times. And I could go like the wind, and they never could catch me. But the last time I escaped, it was 1962. They didn't catch me till 1992. They never gave me no time for escaping. All they do is just get you and bring you back, and that's all. Well, now GOD happened, and because I got this stroke, and 'cause of my knee I can't run no more. It's a waste of a life, it is. I don't really have any people. Since I've been in this prison I've lost 13 members of my family. My mother and father are dead. My sisters are dead. I suppose I have a brother in DALLAS. And that's the only relative that I know I have. I don't have a place to go, but I don't give up. I feel that I can make it ■

"Tex"
WILLIAM HOWARD JOHNSON (67) Theft

well, I was 17 years old, hot headed. My oldest brother had done 14 years in prison and when he got out he had a pretty bad attitude and I was just a kid. He wanted me to accomplish all the things that he never did, so he was pretty hardcore with me. I rebelled against him and life back in Tennessee. I don't know, about six months to a year went by and my mom got real sick and he called and wanted to patch things up. My mom wanted us all to be there 'cause she thought that she was going to die, so I came from Tennessee and moved out here with my parents and my brother.

we started becoming friends, but there was still a lot of tension between us. I was 17, dropped out of school. I was pretty wild. I'd been on my own since I was 12.

It's a long story and a there was a lot of extenuating circumstances to my crime.

But in a nut shell, I got sick and tired of being sick and tired and we got in a hellish argument this particular night, January the 6th. we had been partying since christmas. New Year's and all that. so I was brained and we got to arguing and I said, "I don't need to hear that shit" and he said, "well you goin' to hear it." and I said, "no I'm not goin' to hear it," and before I even really thought of it, I pulled the gun out and shot him. wasted him and proceeded to shoot everybody else that was in the house. I shot my brother, shot my sister-in-law, shot my niece. I didn't know nothing about the law, and all they were talking about was the death sentence, or life without parole. I got the murder, four attempted murders and 1st degree assault. ...

MOOSE
DAVID LOWRY
(30) MURDER, FOUR ATTEMPTED MURDERS, 1ST DEGREE ASSAULT

it's been very hard. it's a nightmare. for a white man it's a nightmare. but i've been honest. told them right off the bat, hey, i didn't mean to do this, it's just rage and i am not trying to escape my responsibility for it. i'm just telling you point blank i just got sick and tired of being sick and tired. i was fed up past my ears and he just threw the last straw in the hay wagon. i believe that everyone of us have that capability within us. you get all kinds of psychological anguish goin' on. shit's goin' crazy in your life and somebody just rubs you the wrong way. murder cases like mine, i'm not saying all of them, but like mine, in the heat of the passion where you just snap and go off, especially at that young of an age, i know i did wrong, there's no doubt about it. if i could wave a magic wand, i would take it back.

"what you feel

Ins

well, you read a lot. you pray a lot and if you are fortunate, you work out as much as you can. you write a lot and are very introspective. i mean i really don't know how to describe it to you in a way that you'd understand. it's just you feel like you don't live anymore, you just exist, you're just filling up space. who you are, what you are, what you feel inside no longer matters; you're just another number.

i believe, in 12 years of being down and knowing a lot of different guys, i believe in my heart, that the solution is in the problem itself.

when i first come in prison, i was as stupid as a box of rocks. i was functionally illiterate. i dropped out of school early on. but goin' to those classes and gettin' the GED (HIGH SCHOOL EQUIVALENCY DIPLOMA), that was the turning point in my life 'cause it made me feel like i could do somethin'. i felt, hell, i'd accomplished somethin', ya know?

i think they need to take guys like myself and a bunch more that i know that's got these heinous murder cases and have shown some stability and shown that they give a shit. i do, that's why i'm here. i came here to work on staff because i wanted to be around older people. i wanted to absorb some of this wisdom. one guy back here in particular, he's dying of lung disease. and he's extremely intelligent and i enjoy listening to him.

seven years now I've maintained a clean record. I've taught for the substance abuse programs. I mean just all round, been a model inmate. I just put in for minimal-out custody, 'cause my attorney told me, "David, you need to get outside the fence and get some trusted time under your belt before you goin' to get parole." so I said OK. I've had minimal-in custody for about three years now. sent in my application, and my record shows me as a very positive inmate, consistently involved in programs, got two jobs, on and on and on. and some guy that don't even know me from Adam writes "unacceptable pattern of violence."

this guy looking in my file, looking at the past record, the violence and all that, but what about the seven years of consistently keeping my nose clean and doing the next right thing? what about that? then he says to my face "unacceptable pattern of violence." far as I'm concerned the violence is stopped. I don't wanta hurt nobody. I just want to go home. want to be with my friends.

what helped me was prayer! this is goin' to sound crazy, but I was at West Jefferson (PRISON), and I was friends with this guy JEFF TAYLOR. this guy served 12 years straight up and was like three or four months before goin' home: no parole or nothin'. He met this girl. Man she was beautiful. They were talking about gettin' married ya know and things were goin' great. There were these guys who were the renegade type, ya know, always wanting to make julep (FERMENTED ORANGE JUICE) and smoke dope and all that kind of stuff. They went to JEFF because they were known violators, so all the time officers shakin' them down. They come to JEFF and wanted to put up some whiskey. He said, "Man, I ain't putt'n up noth'n. I'm trying to go home." They said, "Look man, how you goin' to act? You done turn into the police or what?" so reluctantly, he agreed to put up a five gallon julep in his cell, because police never shook him down.

ide no longer matters"

well, the guys were drunk when he made it and he put hot water in it and killed the yeast. the yeast kinda cooked off. so when they came back three or four days later the whiskey they had put was nothin' but sweet water. when they come back they thought that he had switched their whiskey. They got to arguing and stuff. JEFF steps up on his cell and I heard "boom, boom, boom," fightin' and everythin' and when I look up from the table, JEFF is steppin' outside the door and he's been ripped. His intestines just hangin' down to his knees. I look up and just freak out 'cause I'm close to this dude, and he's looking around trying to hold his guts in, he's looking around like that, and a hand comes out of that big steel door and grabs hold of his hair and snaps it back, WHAM! and his whole throat fell open. The dude took two steps and fell flopping to the floor. Twelve years he did in them fucking hell holes, and to get killed for some bullshit like that! one of the guys, I caught him on the weight pile, skinned him up pretty bad. so they locked me down. . . .

JEFF, he was a good dude, man he was a good dude, and he got wasted for nothin'. After JEFF got killed, I was laying down in my bed, all by myself alone ya know, just thinking, I don't want to go out like this and I never been no bible thumper, spiritual kind of person, I've always kind of believed ya know, always believed there was a higher power. I had a visit with my mom and dad, I'll never forget my dad looked up at me, he said, "son, will you please come home." I never seen my dad cry, but he had a big ol' tear on his face. so you just imagine, goin' back in there, you know that you got 150 years, but your folks don't understand that. I'm going down the hall, the noise and racket, I never will forget it, I walked up into the dormitory, I'm standing up on the rail, looking at them arguing and fussing about dominos, fighting about the phone, just noise man all around just noise, noise, noise and then I go into my room and the walls is closin' in on me, ya know, I mean I feel like I was just about to snap, bust and a couple of hours went by just sitting on the bed. It got dark outside and I never will forget it; I looked out and it was a full moon. That's the way we are. we see, but we see dimly. we don't see the whole picture. That's what got me to think'n spiritually and I didn't know how to address him, BUDDHA, JESUS, or YAHWEH, JEHOVAH, or what. Almighty GOD. If you're out there and you are real and I believe you're out there and I believe you're real and if you are hearing me, please have mercy on my ignorant ass. I got my whole life screwed up and there ain't nothin' I can do. I ain't got no hope. If you're out there and you hear me, if you will please help me, I don't want to make you a whole bunch of promises, but I'm trying to do something beneficial with my life. I think it was the first time I ever experienced peace, peace of mind. Four days later I was transferred from Alabama's most double max security west Jefferson, out of the lock up unit with two disciplinaries hanging over my head to Easterman, a level four goin' home camp. when I got off that van I knew that any given moment folks was goin' to come and grab my arm and say "we made a mistake, computer error, you are not supposed to be here."

"I think it was the first time I ever experienced **peace**'

For the first couple of days, I was just walking around tripping. I'd see genuine smiles, hear little bits and pieces of conversations, "I go up on parole Monday," "I go home on a pass next weekend." I'm hearing all that stuff and guys smilin', playing Frisbee.

I thank GOD to be here 'cause I needed just peace of mind, ya know? Those big camps is constantly just turmoil. Noise. continual noise. You just can't get no peace of mind. Here it's laid back, ya get a lot of older people. It's quiet here. A man can get into some good books, ya know, and get yourself together. That's what I intend on doing anyway. I've got a year before I come for parole. I want to get myself together ∎

It's wondrous what a hug can do.
A hug can cheer you when you're blue.
A hug can say, "I love you so."
Or, "Gee I hate to see you go."
A hug is "welcome back again."
And, "Great to see you! where've you been?"
A hug can soothe a small child's pain
And bring a rainbow after rain.
The hug! There's just no doubt about it—
We scarcely could survive without it.
A hug delights and warms and charms.
It must be why God gave us arms.
Hugs are great for fathers and mothers,
sweet for sisters, swell for brothers.
And chances are your favorite aunts
Love them more than potted plants.
Kittens crave them. Puppies love them.
Heads of state are not above them.
A hug can break the language barrier
And make your travels so much merrier.
No need to fret about your store of 'em;
The more you give the more there is of 'em.
So stretch those arms without delay
And give someone a hug today!

james whitAker (56)

(prison records incomplete)

(32) samuel **Brown**

prison records incomplete

(47) Ervin Jessie

"I ain't done nuthin'
to get in here."

sex crime

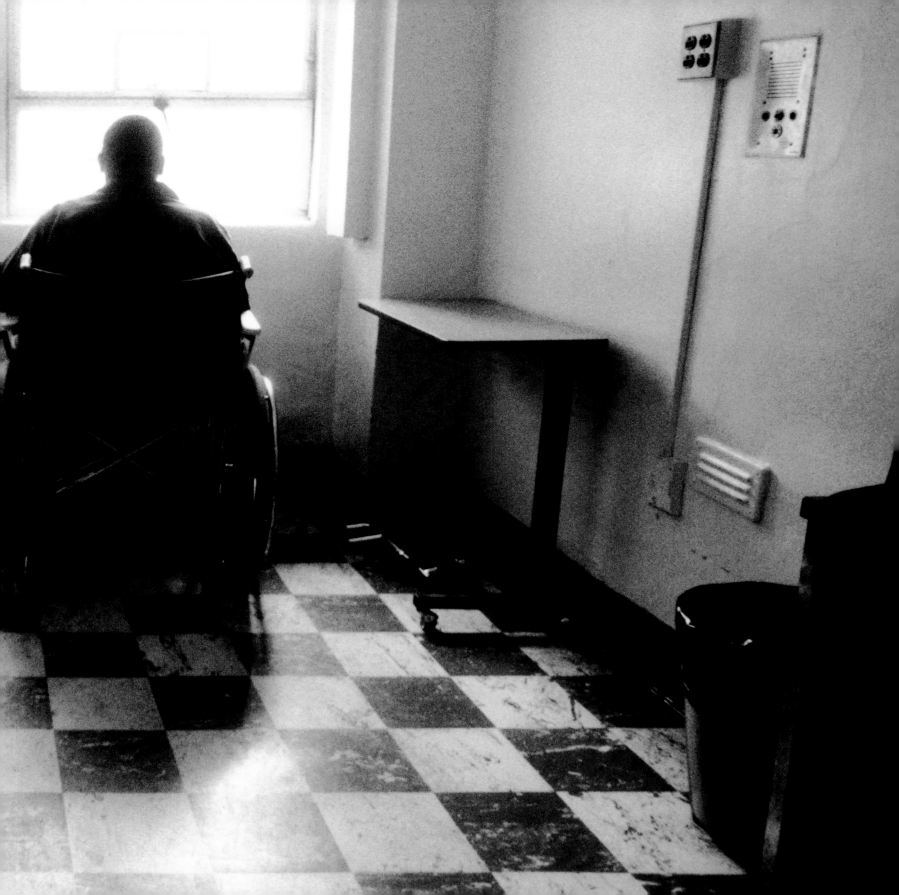

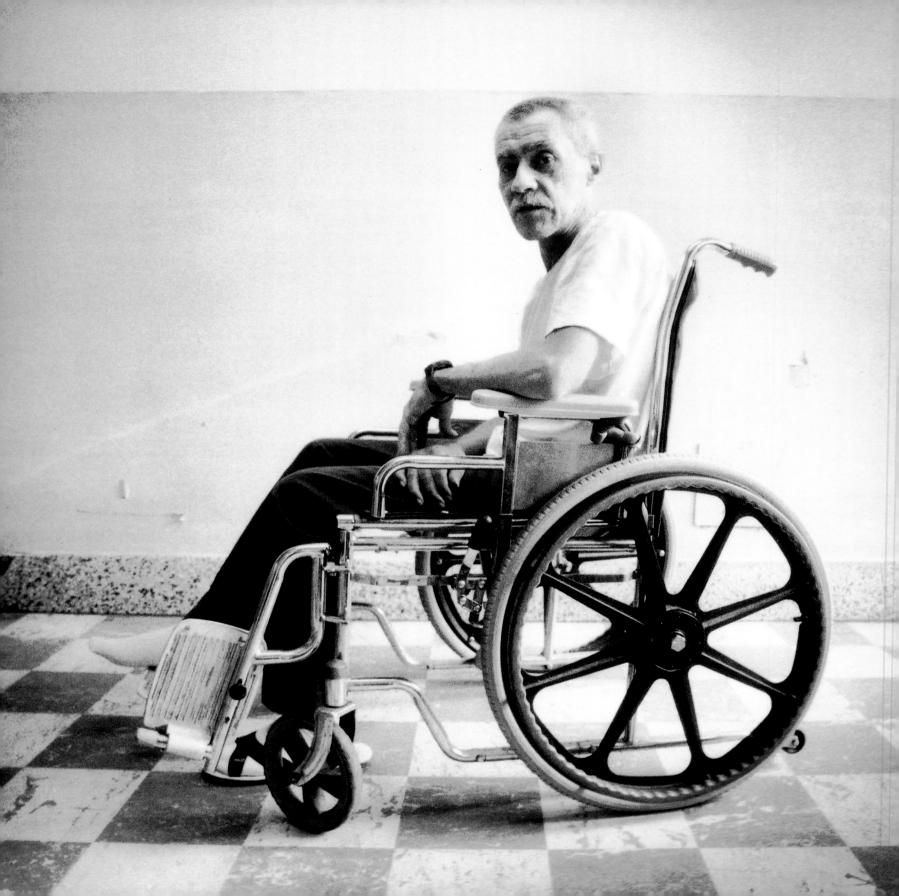

perry (70)

MURDER

pugh

sammy (22)
Habitual offender
gray

I'm 22 years of age. I'm here for burglary, drug running, automobile; stuff like that, mainly non-violent. I got my GED (HIGH SCHOOL EQUIVALENCY DIPLOMA) when I first came down in '91. This is my second time down. But this time I got put up under the habitual offender law. You get a certain age, you look back and see changes which occur—the right choices you could have made. Right now you just think about the wrong things you did. You think about what lies ahead of you and every day I try to better myself. You know, every day is a learning experience, and hopefully I'll be better than I am now. There's a lot of older guys in here... there's some real stuff that they should be ashamed of. And you know, I can look at them and see they got wasted lives and I'm still young. I still have a chance in society. I got a lot of faith in myself. It's nothing to do with the penitentiary or the state of Alabama. Nobody can make you do nothing you don't wanna do. You got to do it for yourself. So you know, just take every day as a learning experience ■

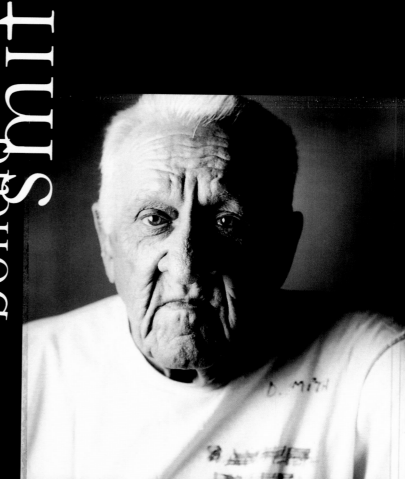

(74) Don Smith

sex crime

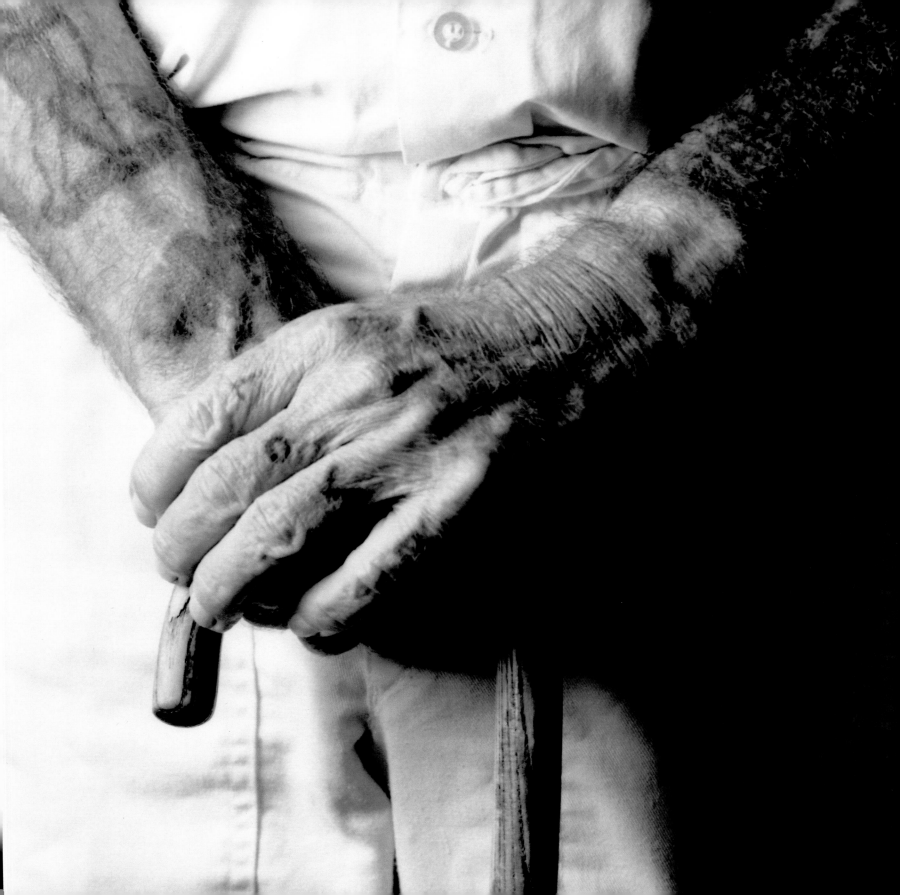

Jackie Gilmer

"I am the chaplain here. It's a volunteer position."

"I believe that surely there is a GOD, there is a devil, and I believe that the devil has trashed everybody's life to some point."

I was selected three and a half years ago when the former chaplain had resigned. The inmates chose me.

I was a visiting minister here at the saturday evening services. I'd been coming for several years and they approached the former chaplain with my name. He called and I came up and met with CAPTAIN ROBERTSON. We talked about my feelings concerning the institution here and so he told me that I had the job. They weren't going to look any further. I put in roughly 20 hours a week here plus my other job.

I'm independent baptist and we believe that once a man comes to CHRIST, he's forgiven and there is no chance of him losing his salvation. He's bound for heaven. GOD, if he's able to forgive your sins, he's able to keep you and see that you make it to HEAVEN.

Over the period of time that I've been here, we've had inmates that professed a knowledge of CHRIST here. They'd get into our bible study and into our teaching ministry here and we've had several that went out and have gotten their lives back together. They've gotten their families back together and it is the success stories that keep you going. We have a lot of failure here, but we also have a lot of success that gets over-looked.

They do fall off the wagon, but you don't give up. You never give up on the person. I believe that surely there is a GOD, there is a devil, and I believe that the devil has trashed everybody's life to some point. Some to a greater degree than others, but I also believe that GOD is a great recycler and he can take what the devil has trashed, recycle it, and turn it out as brand new. So we have to look beyond the outward form of the man we are dealing with, and realize that GOD sees something on the inside of that and he knows what that man could be if he's willing to try. Willing to put forth that effort. And really that's what repentance is. •••

"I've heard some really heartening stories. some guys that don't seem to have a break in their entire life."

Repentance is simply being sorry for what you have done and been willing to turn around and go the other direction, and all of these men are that way.

In this institution alone, I am both loved and hated. It depends on the inmate. where one man sees me as a representative of CHRIST, the other man will see me as a threat. some are looking for excuses and various things but I never shove religion down a man's throat. My first thing is to befriend him. I'll be a friend to anyone and then I'll allow him to open up to me. But it takes time. You've got to be real patient with people.

In my position here, we have dealt with Jewish believers. I saw to it that they had whatever they need for their worship. we have dealt with Muslims. I have a good reputation among the Muslims. we do not discriminate because of a religious belief, but I am not backward or bashful about

telling them that it was the LORD JESUS CHRIST that changed me. I know where I was at in '81. I know the direction I was headed in. I know where I am at today and believe me, where I am at today is a whole lot better than where I was in '81. I don't believe that a man can change on his own. I believe he has to have help. He either has to have help from the human stand-point of the people that will support him and of course the greatest thing would be to get GOD in their lives.

It's hard to live in a place like this. I've heard some really heartening stories. some guys that don't seem to have a break in their entire life. They grew up on the wrong side of the tracks. Their parents were fighting, then their parents were split apart, and their brother had a gun and they went crazy one night and boom, they are in here for 40 years. And you say where is the break in this?

"I was a leader in one of the branches of the klu klux klan here in the state of Alabama and had a hatred for blacks."

I know what it is to be from the wrong side of the tracks, myself. I grew up in an alcoholic home. My dad was an alcoholic. He was gone more than he was there. I won't say what it was, but I had a strong addiction for years myself. I went to work when I was 13. When I reached my late teens and early 20's, I was a leader in one of the branches of the klu klux klan here in the state of Alabama and had a hatred for blacks. A strong hatred for blacks! It was in 1981 that I just felt this empty feeling. I can't explain it, but it was an emptiness. I felt that I had so much hatred built up and so many things had happened through the years that I was ready to commit suicide, and was thinking about it very strongly in the last part of '81. But I will never forget it. It was if God himself touched me and I can't explain it till this day. But I know what I did. I went down to an old pine tree. I knelt down and said "God, if you'll save me and forgive me, I'll serve you the rest of my life." I stood up. I didn't know what to feel because I'd never really been around religion or anything. No real religious background at all, but I stood up. I remembered that I walked maybe 20 feet and it was as if a weight lifted from my shoulders. Literally, like a weight, it lifted and my mind cleared and all the hatred was gone. There's black inmates that you can talk to that's here that know that I was a leader in the klan. I've told them openly, but as much hatred that I had, switched to that much love for people. I don't see the white that these inmates are dressed in. I see the person that's in that. I realize that, that could have been me. All I want to do is tell them that God loves them. God cares. God is not wanting people to suffer like this and to carry this weight and guilt around, but that God loves them ■

cedric (col

(prison records incomplete)

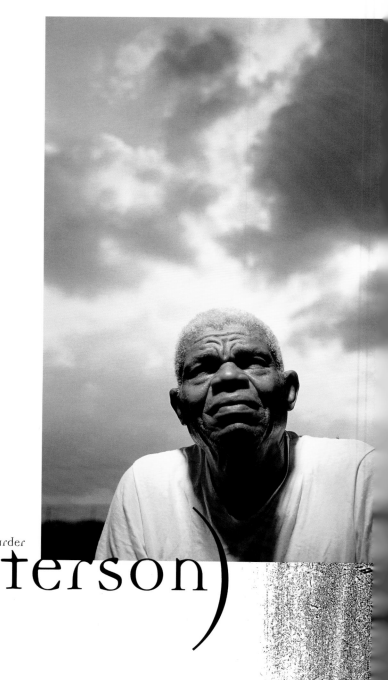

quincy 67 murder
(patterson)

I was born and raised on a farm here in Alabama. I didn't bother with nobody. I wasn't no madman. My mother raised us, and always told us don't pick up no fuss. 'cause if anybody want to fight, try to do the best. And if I'm gonna have to do it, I'm gonna do anything that I have to do. I got run over; I was thrown 132 feet over the car. I broke my leg. I was caught in a fire and burned. I've been shot four times. I been beat up. And I tell you, I just thank the Lord for taking care of me the way he did.

Jesse Hatcher
MURDER (78)

we was good friends. we were drinking whisky and we kinda got mad. if we hadn't been drinking, it would've never happened. I'm very sorry about it, but doesn't do anything now, you know. I'm never gonna get over it though, you know. I'm sorry I did it. But they're the type of people that if you didn't do it to them, they'd do it to you, and I just want to live as long as I can. I have a temper. But I can't help that. I'm not mean or that. I'm not hateful. But I just can't help it. I get to drinking whisky, I couldn't control it, and I just go crazy. I'm as good as gold until I get to drinking. And when I get to drinkin', I'm just like a crazy person. I just can't control it.

I just want to be out like a free man, where I can see my grandchildren, sit down to the table, and tell my children 'bout what I went through and how the Lord has blessed me. But something tells me I'm gonna make it. And I just believe I'm gonna make it ■

(74)
Horru
Nelson
possession and distribution

herschel kunstek

(67) ROBBERY

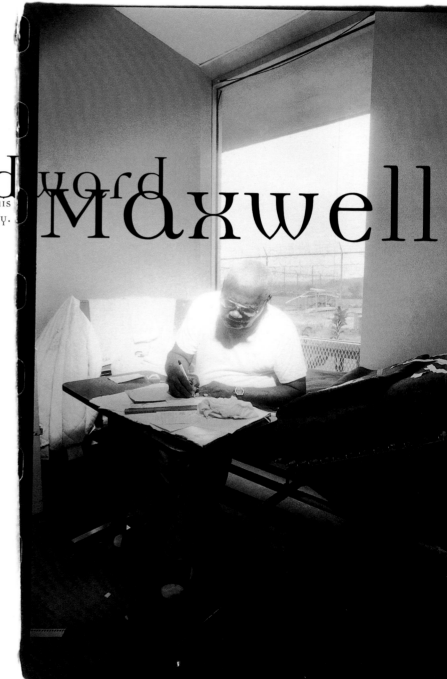

(70) Edward Maxwell

Murdered his fiancee's father in 1955. Now serving his third conviction for robbery.

(82)

Roland Campbell

M U R D E R

Twenty one years ago, I shot a woman.
Killed her. That's about it. Put me in here.
I was young and crazy, had the devil in me...
I wouldn't do nothing like that now.

Drugs is the reason I'm in here. I started on drugs since I was 12 years old. one thing or another. vietnam. that got me in the major leagues. morphine. cocaine. heroin. I was able to walk away from all of that. just before I came in here, I realized that drinking was my trigger to the drugs. I get drunk, I want the rock. And eight years ago, when somebody introduced me to rock. I started it slow, kinda slow. but it was a drug I couldn't turn down. first one I was hooked....

"But it was a drug I couldn't turn down. first one, I was hooked."

michael godfrey (47)
breaking and entering

I always considered myself a strong individual, but when I got a hold of the rock, I couldn't let go. started in on weekends and then it progressed till I had lost all my family but my wife. I went through two jobs because of it. Then finally, five years ago, I had hit what I thought to be my bottom. I turned around and realized I didn't have nobody. couldn't find no more money and nobody else. I had thought I could quit and then on the way home it was like I had lost everything. I walked into the house, and I figured I was gonna lose my wife. I spoke, she wouldn't even turn around to look towards me. I walked in there and grabbed my shotgun off the wall. I couldn't handle life no more. so I took my shotgun and quietly went into my kids' bedroom. I sat down on a chair and I stuck it in my mouth and I went and pulled the trigger, and every time I think about it, it scares the hell out of me, because as I was pulling that trigger a big wave of relief just went over me. I smiled just before I pulled that trigger. I remember just feeling it's finally over, you know? And it clicked. That's the loudest sound I ever heard in my life. But that gun ain't never been unloaded. It had been on that gunrack for six years, and never been unloaded. But the night before my wife unloaded it because my grandson came over. It's six foot up there and my grandson's three foot high. she said that was the reason. But in our talks since then, we realized who actually unloaded that gun. Jesus still had something left here for me to do. what, I don't know yet. He'll tell me in time. But I stayed clean for three years. At first, afterwards, a disappointment rushed over me when she walked in the room and I busted out squalling and it was the first time I've ever in my life asked someone to help me. I was always "I can handle it," but that's the addict, that's the insane part of drugs. But she sat down and put her arms around me and we were both squalling for a little while, and she got on the phone. Just like a trooper. she started making phone calls, but you know there was only one place in NC (NORTH CAROLINA) that we could find, out of all this advertising about helping you with drugs, that would take me without having an insurance policy or a pocket full of money. one place. And I had to admit that I had tried to commit suicide before they would take me. And they put me through a kind of a rehab. It was Good Hope Hospital down here in Irwin. And then after that I put myself into Buttner and straightened myself out. Three years I had a business going. Doing great.

"being put in prison saved my

And then some of them so-called buddies rolled in and I made the mistake that an addict often makes after he'd been clean for about three years. He thinks he's got it under control. I stopped going to meetings. I didn't need them anymore. I had it under control.

All it took was a few drinks of liquor. One of them boys fired that rock up. But that's what brought me in here. I couldn't walk away from that rock. I walked to the door and turned around and called them both sons of a bitch, but I never made it out the door. Turned around back and went "hell, I can handle one. And then I'm going home." $400 in my pocket. My wife waiting on me. And two and a half months later, nobody knew whether I was dead or alive. The county called my wife to say we have your husband down here and he's under arrest for six counts of breaking and entering. I don't remember the first four days of being in jail. About the fourth morning, I got up and I walked and looked in the mirror. I didn't know who the shit that was in that mirror. I was normally about 195 pounds, and I'm five feet 10 inches. I was 130 pounds, eyes with black circles around them and I looked like a raccoon. Eyes sunk back in my head. Cheeks sunk in. Like death warmed over. It scared the hell out of me. But I got back into the program. A lot of people look at me funny when I say that, but I say being put in prison saved my life. It gave me one more chance.

But the mistake I've always made before that I will not make this time, good LORD willing, is I quit for everybody else before. All those times that I quit, I quit for my kids; I quit for my mom; I quit for my dad; I quit for my wife. But I never really wanted to quit. 'Cause I didn't quit for myself. This time it's for me. And with the good LORD's help, it will continue to be for me. I've been two years, eight months and 26 days clean. And I wanna continue doing it one day at a time staying that way. Because this time, I can't stop. I can't really ever remember wanting this 'cause I've never really been straight long enough, but I wanna see what Michael can do. What he can accomplish. Without drugs. I've always wondered that, to see how far I could go, if I was given the chance. Now I've been given the chance. Now I gotta be the man. 'Cause the LORD's given me a whole lotta chances now, and I've got a real good feeling that this may be my last one. •••

life."

"we want the kids to know what the family

when I get outta here, I've got a goal. It's a small goal. An addict never sets a big goal. 'cause there's always a chance of disappointment. And that's the road right back to drugs. You make little goals. when you accomplish that goal, it helps you, builds your confidence for the next goal. But I have got a goal when I get outta here. Me and my wife want to try something. Addicts always talk to kids at schools, talk to them at meetings, but it's always been the addict alone, showing only his side. we want the kids to know what the family goes through. That'll be the double whammy, eye opener for those kids. 'cause some kids, and I was one of 'em, will listen to them addicts, but then they'll say, "well it's my life, and if I wanna do it, it's my business." But if them kids know that it ain't just their life that they'll be screwing up, it's gonna be their momma, their daddy, their brothers and possibly their kids, like I did my three kids. Then maybe if I can help one, just one, it'll have been all worth it. Every damn bit of it. I'd do it again, just if I could help one ■

goes through."

gary pinyon (50)

MURDER

I was an auto-body repairman. I used to work for the sheriff's department, too. I got involved with a married woman and she was having problems with her husband. Marital problems. She was wanting rid of him. So she asked me to help her. She finally convinced me after about a year to get somebody to do it. I was a bouncer at this time and I knew a lot of people. I met some folks there who had some connections. I made a few phone calls and he was history. I never did anything else in my life except that, and I really don't know why. I have a weakness for people in trouble. I saved officers' lives. I saved a woman's life down in florida while I was down there. There's a lot of good people out there who helped me. People came in and gave statements. And not one said a bad thing about me, even my ex-wife. Everybody liked me and I guess they were just so surprised ∎

STABBED HIS MOTHER 47 TIMES OVER A LAUNDRY DISPUTE

"I'm a WWII veteran and I have what they call a mad passion. when I get mad, I just go ahead and kill. but now it's different. I feel altogether different." **hamiltom a+i correctional officer speaking of WALKER SMITH:** WALKER SMITH was working on his mother's washing machine and she kept giving instructions and I think it was more than WALKER could handle, and he just took the kitchen knife and stabbed her to death on the spot. WALKER don't get a whole lot of outside support. mainly what he gets is within the institution. and if you'll notice WALKER now, most of what he possesses he wears around his neck. and if it breaks for any reason, he's back at me wanting another chain. y'know I'll try to oblige him if I can, 'cause that's all he has. that's all his possessions is what he wears around his neck. everything else belongs to the state of Alabama ■

walker smith (76) murder

martin upchurch
(63) BUYING STOLEN GOODS

john williams

Burglary

(54)

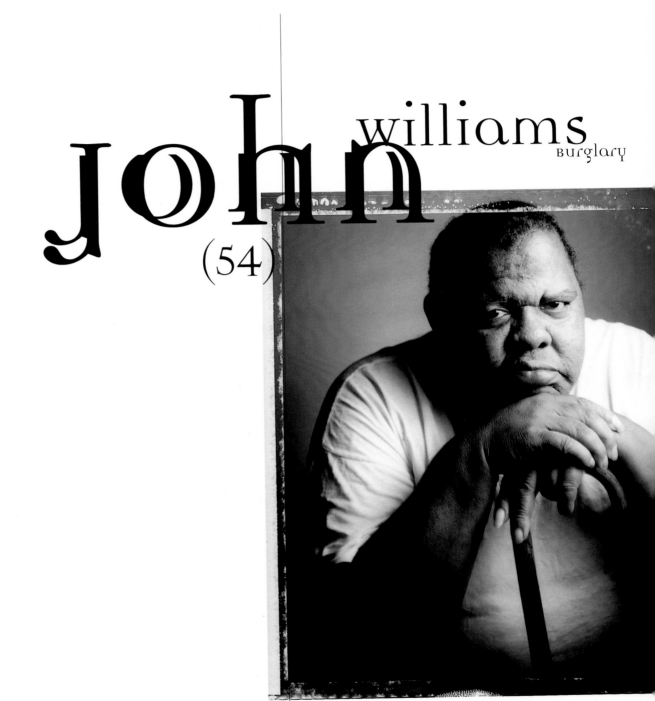

Basically, when this place opened in '81, it included work release and A+I (AGED AND INFIRM) inmates. Our population for A+I at the time was 64, something like that, whereas now it's increased to big numbers. As far as we knew, this is the first A+I at the time. When we began to operate this as an A+I facility there were no SOP's (STANDARD OPERATING PROCEDURES), there was no administrative regulations, so the situation as it came up, day after day, was new territory. How to employ these inmates, what to do with them as far as meals, visiting and what kind of procedures we'd set up to deal with the handicapped versus the chronically ill, etc. There was just a whole array of different problems that came up that had to be solved all the time.

We have inmates here who are totally dependent upon someone else to care for them. Cleaning, bathing, getting them up, getting them down. I think somewhere in the system, in the judicial system, there needs to be a set of guidelines established to deal with those inmates. They're no longer a threat to anyone. There's no program in the system to look at these people individually and determine whether or not we can return them to society without any stress on it. What it is, it's a big expense on the state trying to maintain people like that. A tremendous expense. Medical care, dental. Anything that's involved with such a situation. And equipment, wheel chairs and all kinds of things that they need. So that's one thing that I think the state could look at. Although there's not that many of them but still it's a program that they need to look at that could save us in the long run lots of money.

I don't know how many life without parole inmates we have in Alabama, but we have a habitual law in Alabama. Three time loser law. A lot of folks are sentenced to life without parole based on their crime. You can relate somewhere back in their history every one of these back to drugs, alcohol or women. Usually, it's going to be one of those three or a combination that bring them in here to begin with. So our prisons are filling up with those kind of folks and they can't do nothing but get older. So this place can't do nothing but grow.

captain (Joe Robertson (FOREFRONT)

It's to the point right now where growth is necessary. Either here or another facility someplace. The convenience of this place is that everything that they need in order to get their life in line is all under one roof, and they don't have to worry a bit.

We had these two inmates, both of them had chronic medical problems; one being a lung disorder, the other a heart condition. So they managed to come up with the tools to cut through the fence on the west side of the facility and made their getaway. They were gone about 15 minutes, and by the time that they had got as far as the hospital, which is across the street, they were exhausted to the point where they went into the emergency room and checked themselves in. They asked to get us over here to come and get them. Because they were beyond any limit of escape at that point. We simply walked over there and brought them back inside the facility ∎

As my life fades away
in an Alabama prison cell
I wonder how this came to pass
being in this living hell.
I worked hard for 40 years
and helped the ones in need
I shared what I had with others
I never believed in greed.
And then one day a tragedy
in my life did entail.
A jealous ex-wife of my only son
had me thrown into jail.
She swore lies, and her sister too
and they had me put away.
So I'll be here till the day I die
as my life fades away.

truman purdy
"Thunderhawk"

They told me when I come in here, you're no longer a citizen. That first really knocked the fire outta me, y'know? And then I said, well, maybe that's the best thing. They said, you're the property of Alabama. You're no longer a citizen of the United States. And, boy, I thought about it. The more I've seen going on, when I do... I'll probably never live to get out of here, unless something comes along and somebody helps me, 'cause the way they got it set up, I can't get out of here, I can't never get out of here. But anyway, if and when I ever did get out of here, I would go to another country, change my citizenship. I wouldn't live in the United States ■

(63) sex crime

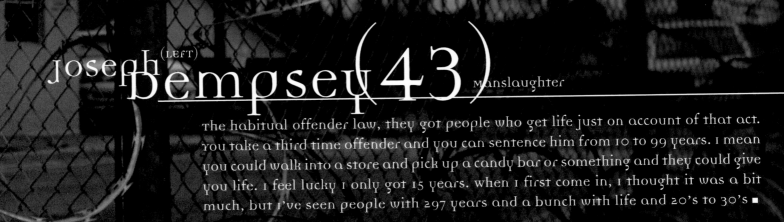

joseph (LEFT) **bempsey** (43) Manslaughter

The habitual offender law, they got people who get life just on account of that act. you take a third time offender and you can sentence him from 10 to 99 years. I mean you could walk into a store and pick up a candy bar or something and they could give you life. I feel lucky I only got 15 years. when I first come in, I thought it was a bit much, but I've seen people with 297 years and a bunch with life and 20's to 30's ■

Earl anderson (59) sex crime (CENTER)
Kim butler (37) sex crime (RIGHT)

trafficking Robert **(75)**
Cowlin

well, conditioning will make you do most things. couldn't make ends meet. I needed money to pay for my wife's doctor bills, hospital bills. we were both sick. she's in the hospital now. she's got an operation on her legs. can't walk around, but she's doing pretty good ∎

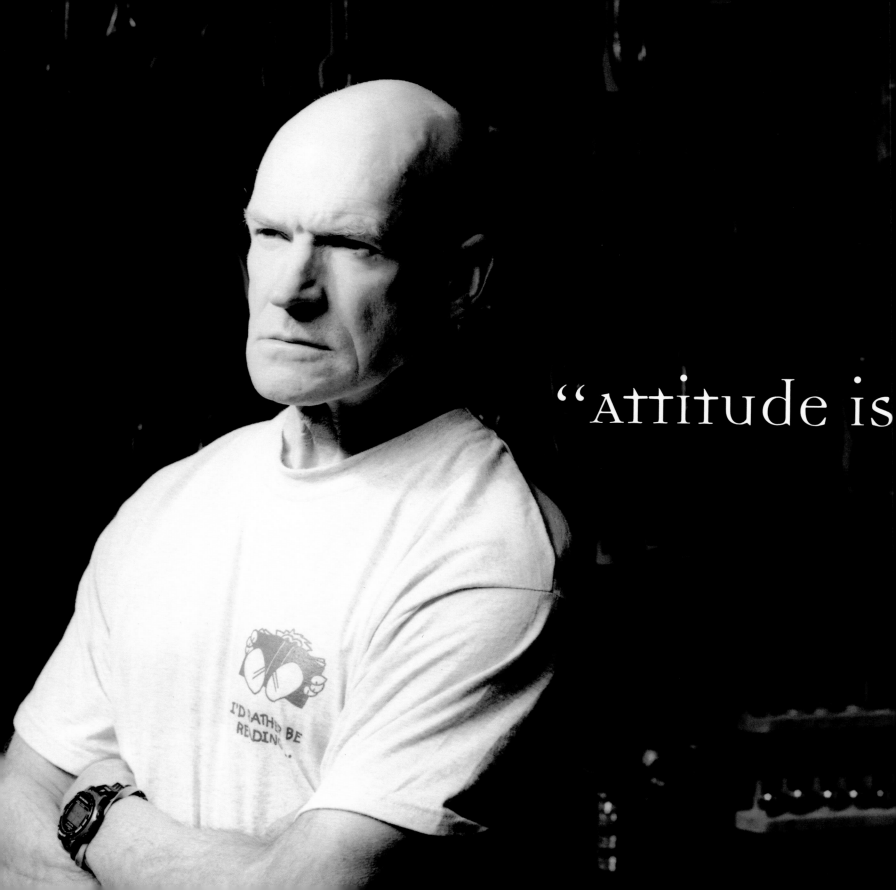

"attitude is

everything.

you survive with the proper attitude.
you go under with the wrong attitude."

I was a specialist in what is known as physical medicine and rehabilitation. I also have a degree and am fully qualified to practice law. I was dealing in millions of dollars in terms of possible disability. some of these cases were absolutely insoluble. some of the people, with all due respect, were totally non-facile with English. I was dealing with interpreters, some of whose judgments, I was less than sure of in terms of what they were saying. I had to sift through mounds of stuff that accumulated over the years in terms of seeing docs, seeing physiotherapists, chiropractors, psychiatrists, whatever, and in short, it drove me to my wits end, and I just went off it and I reacted against my wife. "BOOM." moments before the tragedy occurred, she hugged me and you know... that's why I'm here.

I had to keep working to keep my head above water. It was just these ridiculous and elaborate investments in real estate, meaning it was $7,500 a month just to cover that, let alone my secretary, office expenses, whatever. so I was up to here financially and I was dealing with this sort of stuff and I just broke, in a nutshell.

There's no way I can make reparations to my victims, least of all my wife and her family, but what I do in here and what I do subsequently outside, either honors or dishonors my victims. I believe in that strongly ■

ROBERT MCKNIGHT (58) MURDER

charles Brewer (30) SEX CRIME

(prison records incomplete)

Jimmy
(56)
Haynes

emmett muncher. theft (57)

Amos "Famous Amos" C. Evatt. fraud (58)

Truman "Thunderhawk" purdy. sex crime (63)

charles brewer. sex crime (30)

kenneth Richardson (prison records incomplete)

(55)chandler

HENRY

S E X U A L T

Harvey Joe Tr han (49) Murd

william hanks

murder(49)

stabbed his father to death

James penn
(62) MURDER

"you can become addicted to money..."

I was involved in a murder due to the fact that a party that I was with had stolen some money. And there was an altercation between she and I, and we were in my aunt's home and during the altercation between she and I, my aunt came in and at some particular time, I really blinked. I don't know what really happened, but I went to stab the girl about the money, due to the fact that she said that she didn't take it. Instead my aunt jumped between us at that particular time and I stabbed her instead. And she died. It was proven in court that it was an accident. I was supposed to be charged with manslaughter but instead they charged me with 2nd degree murder. So therefore I received a life sentence. I had no reason because I loved my aunt. We were best friends. She raised me and there was no reason that I would've had any animosity towards her in any way. I lost more than I could ever gain, because, as I said, she was my friend as well as my aunt. Like I say, I would be willing to give my life if it would bring her back. But GOD in heaven knows that it wasn't an intentional thing, and the person I was trying to hurt testified to that in court and told them exactly how close my aunt and I was. I lost two homes and I lost two automobiles and I lost all my personal property due to drugs. I worked in the post office, I worked in a NAVY research laboratory in washington, D.C., I worked at a microbiological science lab in Bethesda, Maryland, and I stayed in the Marine corp for seven years—and I lost all of this due to drugs. Not taking them, but the fast money. Because you can become addicted to money as well as you can drugs. I wouldn't advise anyone to take a chance on selling drugs. I would much rather work for minimum wage now. I lost retirement when I could have drawn it if I had stayed. I lost my family. I lost everything that I had. I believe that one day that I'll walk out of here a free man and I'll be able to tell a lot of people about the mistake that I made, and hopefully if I can keep just one person from getting involved in drugs, I'll feel good about myself, because like I say, you've got nothing to gain and everything to lose ■

MANSLAUGHTER

billy dunn

6 5)

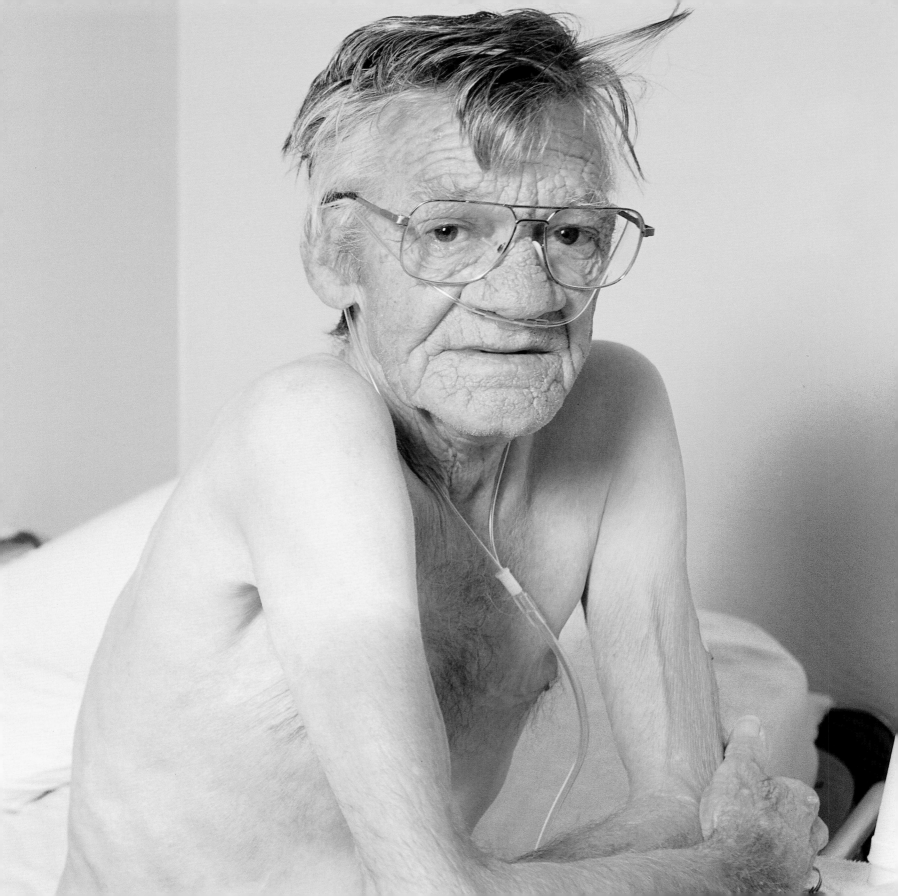

i'd never been inside a county jail. when i first walked in i saw an inmate that looked like ARNOLD SCHWARZENEGGER and i looked around and i had second thoughts, but i'd already received a broken neck and said this job's not going to beat me, so i stuck it out. that was 14 years ago.

(officer) ronald contrel

in a large institution, when i worked there, there were 1,700 inmates. it was, at that time, the largest in the state. it was maximum security. you had dangerous inmates. it was tension. a lot of tension. you didn't have to worry so much about the inmates attacking you, they would attack each other. there were officers that were getting assaulted occasionally, but the biggest majority of assaults were inmates upon other inmates. in prison it is a society unto itself. the strong survive. they pick. they have the gangs. they have the Aryans. they have the Black panthers. they have the Muslims. they have all different groups and they are opposing each other. the strong survive. the weak are preyed upon. they are taken advantage of. All manner of things happen to them.

you catch what you can. you do what you can. you can't catch it all because they have a system that's called the "hotgriddle" system. when they are doing something that they are not supposed to be doing, and they have another fellow over here and another fellow over there, and when they see officers coming they go to the door and yell "hotgriddle." well that automatically tells them that the officers are coming, so they stop whatever they are doing. you catch some of it, but you can't catch it all ∎

Jesse "Hitman" Kitchens (61)

I came down to see a man at his house in Alabama and pumped two bullets into his chest. He was mixed up in the marijuana trade, alcohol business. It was what I was told to do, I guess, by people in Georgia. He got some money somewhere and double-crossed ol' Honest Eddy. I'm the only one they put in a penitentiary. The others got away with their shit ∎

melvin thomas (63) attempted murder

charged with shooting into a house of a neighbor after an argument over a road easement.

gary kinsey (50)

NARCOTICS POSSESSION

They put me in here because I have a lot of medical things that are wrong. I have an enlarged heart. pancreas don't work. I'm a diabetic and I had a stroke the 1st of this year. They give me Anacin. That's about it. I was scheduled before the sentence to have open heart surgery to take care of the three blockages that I have. But the judge didn't see fit to wait for that long, and so I have to wait until the sentence is over, a year along ■

while attempting a robbery "TEX" was shot in the back by an officer. The force of the bullet pushed his intestines, kidney, and stomach out through the abdominal wall.

LUVErn "TEX" raylor (67)

Burglary

They operated on me and they didn't tell me... they put a plastic stomach in me and it bust open in Holman (PRISON).

franklin Earl Humphrey (60)

1 MURDER

FOUND HIS WIFE WITH HER LOVER,
SHOT HIM IN BED

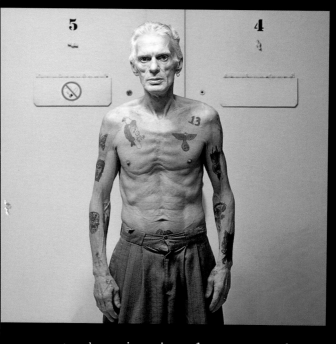

I've been in prison for 35 years for robbery and attempted murder. I started stealing when I was 15. I robbed banks. I always worked alone. In 1994, I was caught for attempted murder. I had mixed booze and medications. Eight months ago I got married to a woman my age and it's going well. That's why I want my release, to live with her. In 1996 I got lung cancer. Now, I'm getting treated but they won't release me. They're waiting for me to die. I lost 50 pounds since October 1999. I regret commiting the crime that sent me here, but I think the system isn't fair for the situation I'm living in now. There should be improvements. Especially when someone has cancer. They should let them go live with their family. I was twice refused conditional release. There's a group that's trying to do something for me. I hope they'll be successful ∎

sauvageau
jules (59)
Attempted murder

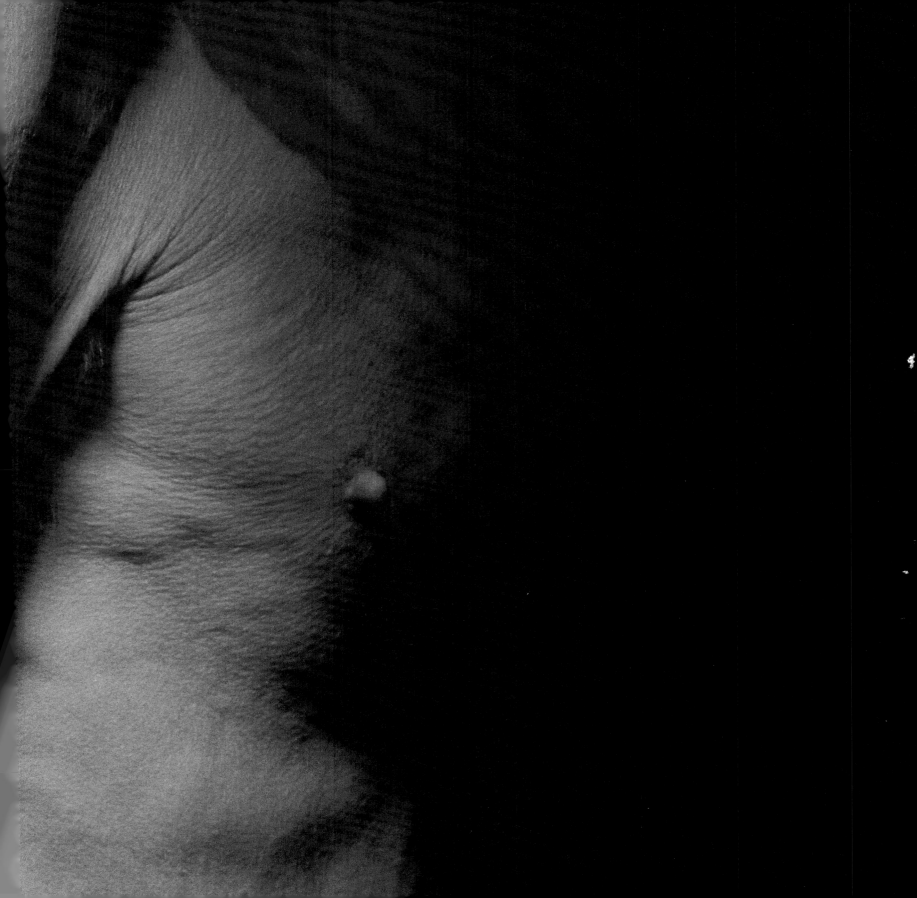

gary crutchfield

(assistant superintendent for programs)

look at murder and life sentences. nationwide, the statistics of actual time served in prison for murder on a life sentence was six years and 10 months. a lot of times, you see people that have committed a lot of other things and they finally led up to murder. we had 25,783 people that were murdered in 1996 in the united states. we only had 14 people that were executed last year. i'm not saying that people should be locked up and throw away the key, but we have to have enough punishment in our laws to make a person never want to break the law again.

our society's turned into the proverbial frog. he's cold-blooded. put him in the little pen of water. if it's the same temperature as his body, he won't jump out. if you just gradually turn it up a half a degree every minute or so, he won't notice the change of temperature, but over time he will sit right there in that little pen of water until he's boiling to death. and i think that we keep weakening things in our laws, that eventually we're gonna have to get tough in order to protect society, because society right now is hiding behind security locks and bolts and bars on their windows. they're the ones who are becoming incarcerated. i mean, i look at some of the saudi arabia-type countries and their tolerance for crime is just no tolerance for it at all and we call them barbaric. like if they cut someone's hand off for stealing a watch, that's inhumane treatment, but they only have to do that about three or four times a year. and they don't have to worry about crimes. and what's more barbaric, to have one out of every four women in the country raped and 25,000 people a year murdered, or to really get tough on crime? we're just not tough enough to get anybody's attention. ....

I've worked with the young, and those type of offenders are much more challenging to work with than the geriatric inmate. They usually have fairly extensive crime records. They pretty much have done everything they're going to do. Youth surprised the heck out of me. I had guys on my caseloads at 15 committing murders. It's kind of an eye-opener for you because you didn't think that a child or kid of 15 has the potential to take a shot gun, shoot somebody with it and get involved with things that they do. We got a lot of rapes and stuff. Twelve year olds raping girls that are five or six; I've had those on my caseloads.

But the geriatrics, they don't have anything to prove. They're not beating their chests, going, "I'm a man." I guess they've matured enough, their throats are big enough that they don't have to feel that they have to prove anything. Plus they just don't have the energy to do just a whole lot of backing up talk and stuff because they're not in shape and they're winded. Your geriatric inmates are going to be child molesters, drug dealers and murderers. That's basically it. That's their crime of choice. They're not going to be breaking and entering because they're too old to toss the TVs out of the windows, much less climb in and out of them. It's just a physical thing.

Inmates are doing stuff these days that, 15 or 16 years ago, was not heard of. The older inmates that were in the system, they had their own code of ethics. The newer inmates, the young inmates today have no respect for authority. They don't respect their parents, they don't respect their teachers, they don't respect officers.

"we have a handful a year tha

We've gotta start where kids are kids and it's going to take involvement from the parents and husbands in the family. Getting active and involved with the kids. Leading them and listening to them. Don't just teach them how to walk, teach them where to walk. More discipline, more understanding, more time spent with them. Because if we're not there to do it, somebody else is gonna be there to teach them. And they're learning from older kids and all the bad influences. North Carolina has got its own problems. We're not a very wealthy state when you look at average incomes compared with the rest of the states. And if you look at the amount of working mothers, we're one of the top ones in the nation, and if you look at education, we're down there near the bottom. They're all in crime. NC was number one or two in the nation for locking up people and all of these things are interrelated. And it starts at the home and in the family. There's no program out there that can replace the parent.

We had an inmate, SANFORD BROOKS, escape. He's way on up there age-wise, close to 80, I guess. He ran out when an 18-wheeler tried to get through the front gates, and he ran in between the gates, and he hardly got past the parking lot, when we got him. Of course, he was already out of breath. It wasn't even something to worry about.

we had another one escape. He just left the rehab therapy department, went down the hill and I actually think he was trying to come back when they got him. The truth is it was dinner time and he was about 150, 200 yards away from the prison when they got him. He was heading that way anyway. He was probably 75. One of the staff people was chasing him. And he was running towards the prison!

We're pretty good about catching inmates. We had one escape not long ago. And it was the one place we did not look, which was the front gate. He just came back to the front gate. He was walking toward the front gate when we actually caught him. He couldn't wait to get back.

We have a handful a year that just absolutely refuse parole. We've got some that are institutionalized. Been here since early 1952. And they won't even go outside the prison to the rehab programs. Or the therapy programs. They won't go to recreation. They won't even leave the compounds of the prison. They're institutionalized big-time and this is home for them. The only time they act up is if you start to talk about trying to get them a home plan or put them in a nursing home.

just absolutely refuse parole."

There will have to be more elderly prisons. One thing that did happen that was good with structured sentencing was the fact that they took a life sentence and made it for murder a 25 year sentence. Before, you could be eligible for parole. If you look at the fine print, after 25 years, they have to go back before a superior court judge in the sentencing county for recommendation to the governor's office for parole. At least they have to do 25 years now. 25 years, minimum. The other thing, too, I really wish they'd get serious about sex crimes, because women getting raped the way they are. We're just not tough enough at all. And you start getting people's attention on that and then I think we'll have a little bit safer society. Even child molestation, it's a joke. We're not near serious enough with the punishment for rape and child molestation. I think those are a couple of areas we just need to throw the book away. And just take care of business.

About 33 percent of the ones we have in McCain Hospital that are geriatrics are child molesters. Who knows how long it's been going on. Most of the time, of course, it's either a family member or somebody you did know. It's not like they're just grabbing kids.

We have sex offender treatment programs. But everything I've ever seen in statistics, shows that even with treatment, 85 percent will re-offend within three years. There's almost no hope for it. And it makes me wonder, if the statistics are that high, what about the other 15 percent? Were they really success cases? Or was it that they just didn't get caught? ∎

MURDER **(51)** JASON RILEY

Hamiltom A+I correctional officer speaking of JASON RILEY: That's a desperate kind of fellow, I believe. cannot, should not, be released out into the population. If there's anything close to what we'd call a serial killer at this facility, between us, JASON RILEY is one of them. He goes beyond murder out of passion for whatever reason. He likes to cut 'x's and this kind of stuff to... breasts... so there's a problem there. The only reason he's here is because he's legally blind. Legally blind don't mean he has to walk around with a stick, but he's limited visually somewhat. so that's the only reason he's here. otherwise, he would be in the heart of the institution somewhere. A big institution. He don't ever want to go to florida. He committed the same kind of crimes as in Alabama. And I think they're looking at doing away with him down there, if they could get their hands on him ∎

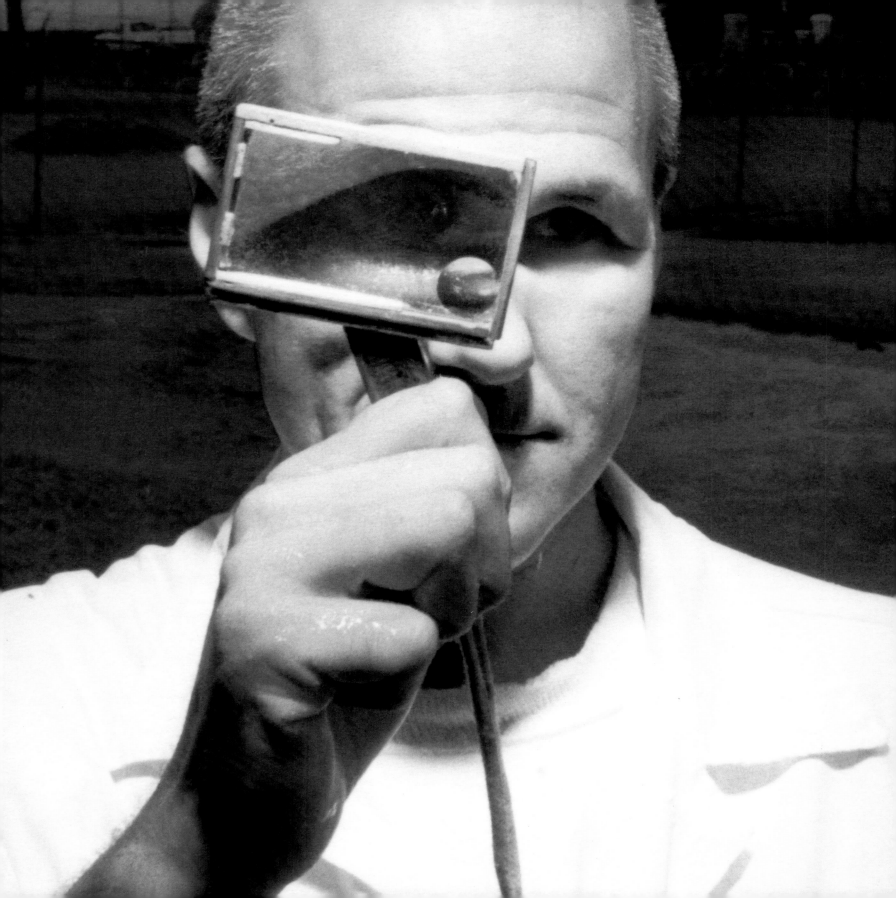

"I'm 23 years old, and been to prison twice in the state of Alabama. well, down south a black man ain't got too much of a chance."

TORY minson

TRAFFICKING

(23)

marcel carrière (73) murder

My first sentence was in 1947 for robbery. But I came back often after that (NINE TIMES). All small sentences. The one I'm serving now is for murder; it's my second murder conviction. The first one, I had killed a woman and was sentenced for life. I was eligible for release after 10 years and got out the year after. I was free for a few months, then I killed another man. I had gotten mad after he refused to give me a job as a janitor and I killed him with a hammer. Then I took him to the garage. I cut off his hands, his feet and his head. I then put everything in green bags and it was picked up with the garbage.

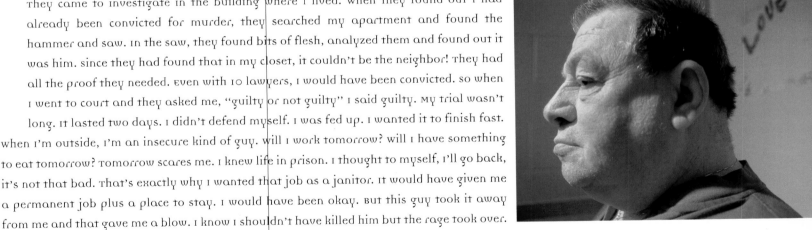

They came to investigate in the building where I lived. When they found out I had already been convicted for murder, they searched my apartment and found the hammer and saw. In the saw, they found bits of flesh, analyzed them and found out it was him. Since they had found that in my closet, it couldn't be the neighbor! They had all the proof they needed. Even with 10 lawyers, I would have been convicted. So when I went to court and they asked me, "guilty or not guilty" I said guilty. My trial wasn't long. It lasted two days. I didn't defend myself. I was fed up. I wanted it to finish fast. When I'm outside, I'm an insecure kind of guy. Will I work tomorrow? Will I have something to eat tomorrow? Tomorrow scares me. I knew life in prison. I thought to myself, I'll go back, it's not that bad. That's exactly why I wanted that job as a janitor. It would have given me a permanent job plus a place to stay. I would have been okay. But this guy took it away from me and that gave me a blow. I know I shouldn't have killed him but the rage took over.

Soon, I'm going to minimum. They organize group outings with a staff member. They take drives into town. I'd like to see a bit of something before I die. Even at my age, I'd rather be walking on saint catherine street (MONTREAL) than in the courtyard here. But I have to pay for what I did. I'd like to tell the young people not to get involved in anything... especially not drugs. That's the plague today. I have four kids; three girls and a boy. They take drugs. I can't stand drugs. I saw enough things happening with drugs, even in prison. So I told them, when you stop taking drugs, you can come to see me. Myself, I've never done drugs. You can say that I ruined my life. I wish I could start over again with the experience that I have. It wouldn't be the same ∎

The biggest problem is too much alcohol. It'll make you do weird things. such as going into DT's and getting in more troubles than you can get out of. Me and my old lady got separated and were going through a divorce and I started to get drunk all night. stay drunk all night, stay drunk about a month and wound up in a DT. I got three life sentences in '85 ■

"Has this place changed me? (Nah.'

George Lavelle Brooks (57)
(prison records incomplete)

bailey

(62) Alexander

"I'd advise everybody to stay out."

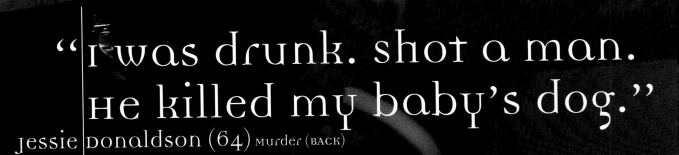

"I was drunk. shot a man. He killed my baby's dog."

jessie Donaldson (64) murder (BACK)

lavon alford (62) attempted murder (FOREFRONT)

I was off in a barroom in mobile (ALABAMA), got into an argument with a bartender and he knocked me off of a stool with a pool stick. I fell onto the floor bleeding, and he came out from behind the bar with a club standing over me. He was telling and cussing me to get up. And I said, "No I'm not going to get up. I'm gonna send something back to you." I happened to have a .38 in my pocket, I pulled the .38 and shot him twice. He lived. but I got 15 years penitentiary. what started it all, he called my wife a bitch. she was with me. My wife was trying to get me to go home and I told her I wanted one more drink. Then the bartender got into it, and then my wife told him to mind his business and he told her, "you shut up bitch." And then I took it from there.

I had somebody ask me sometime if my case was alcohol-related. I said, "well, it happened in a bar." They said, "well, it's alcohol-related." I said, "well, what if it would have happened in the parking lot of wal-mart. would you say it was wal-mart-related?" They blame everything on alcohol ∎

"I'm drawn to work with people who are either marginalized or minorities. people who do not really have a voice."...

Marie Andrée Drouin

(seventeen years in corrections. five years as warden of grand valley institution for women, in kitchener, ontario. director of the newly created division, established in november 1999, for geriatric inmates.)

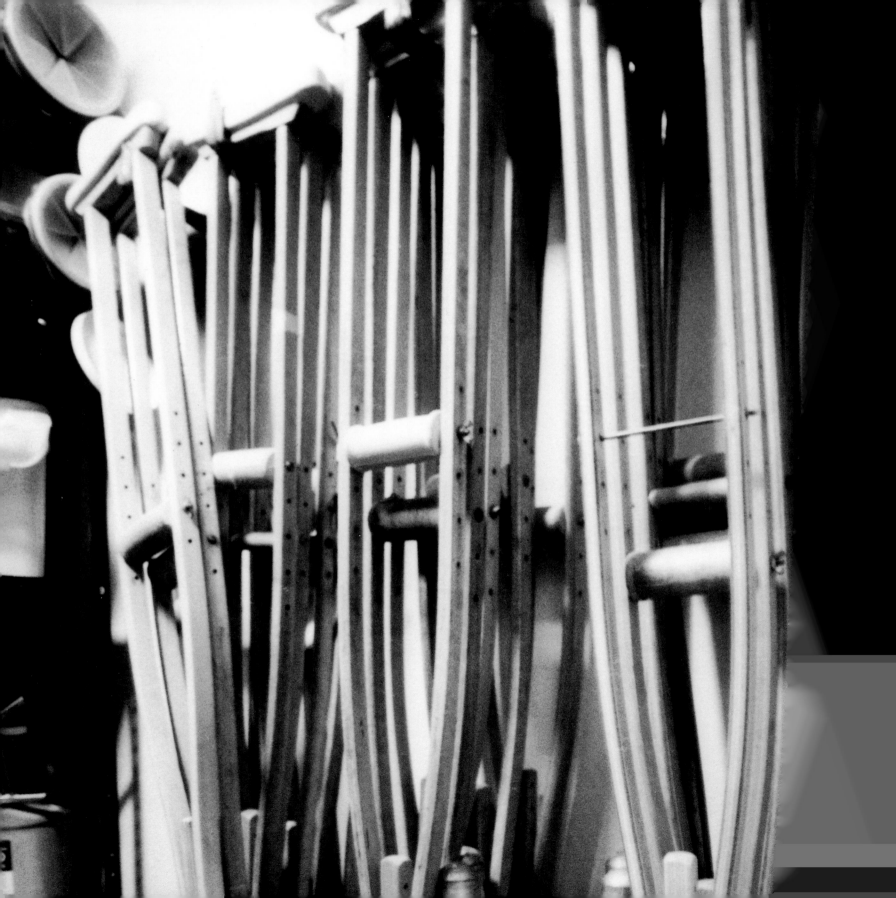

i believe that older offenders do not belong in the mainstream of corrections. they have special needs. we've been saying this for 10 years and i believe it's time to do something about it.

There's no question in my mind, we need to reform the court system. ultimately we have to look at alternatives to incarceration for many of these people. they should not even come into our facilities. The reality is that 72 percent of our older folks are coming into the system for the first time. These people have led a pro-social lifestyle for much of their life.

i believe there are 50,000 older offenders in the states. For us in canada it's 4,000 out of roughly 21,000. so it's like 17 percent. in the states it's four percent out of two million inmates. so there's a big difference in terms of proportions. For us, it needs to be making a difference in the way we do business.

every decision we make should be based on risk. That's what our mandate is. to assess risk, to manage risk, and to prevent further criminal behavior. well, when you see someone who is just ready to die, how much risk do they present? we should be able to manage them in the community.

some of these people would welcome electronic monitoring. they say, 'well, we have no difficulty of being accountable for our whereabouts, but we would like to be in an environment that would be good for us.' I do believe that we have way too many of these people in the incarceration part of our system. we should feel that more of them go directly to the community and also contribute back—restorative justice—because a lot of these people have amazing skills. they've been on the outside for most of their lives. what would prevent them from being care-givers—going to seniors' homes and helping out, depending, obviously, on their crime. going to places where people have physical disabilities and helping.

we have initiated a care-giver program in some of our institutions where middle-age offenders look after the elderly or people with HIV/AIDS, or other types of infectious diseases. they look after them 24 hours a day. when they are released to the community, what we are trying to do is release them at the same time, so that they can continue to help them in the community. it does wonders, because the care-givers feel that, for the first time for many of them, they are put in a position where they can actually assist someone else. they are responsible to improve the day of some of these frailer inmates. it heals them through helping others. it also teaches them to look after themselves. instead of becoming frustrated and angry and bitter, they learn a lot of stuff, from how to lift a patient, to massage, to aroma therapy. it's also about companionship, security and comfort, and sometimes just sharing a nice laugh. we're looking to see if we can accredit the program. since the population is aging internationally, these people may be interested in pursuing a career in that field.

"for older folks, it's to help them age with dignity and die with dignity."

I would like to see most of the older offenders in minimum security. but I would like all the medium and minimum institutions to have a designated unit, to have a living area that would provide all these people to age in place. for example, if they're healthy they would continue to be involved in mainstream activities, mix with the other population. but as they age and become more frail, they would have access at that institution to different levels of care so that they would not have to be moved from one institution to another. I think that they should be removed from the mainstream for their personal safety.

many of them will be with us for a long time. many of them may actually pass on while they are in our care. in corrections in canada, we often hear from our commissioner that offenders are sent to prison as punishment, not for punishment. our mandate is not to make it hard for them. for most inmates, it's to give them what they need so that they can acquire the skills, and amass the tools they need to actually return as law-abiding citizens. for older folks, it's to help them age with dignity and die with dignity ■

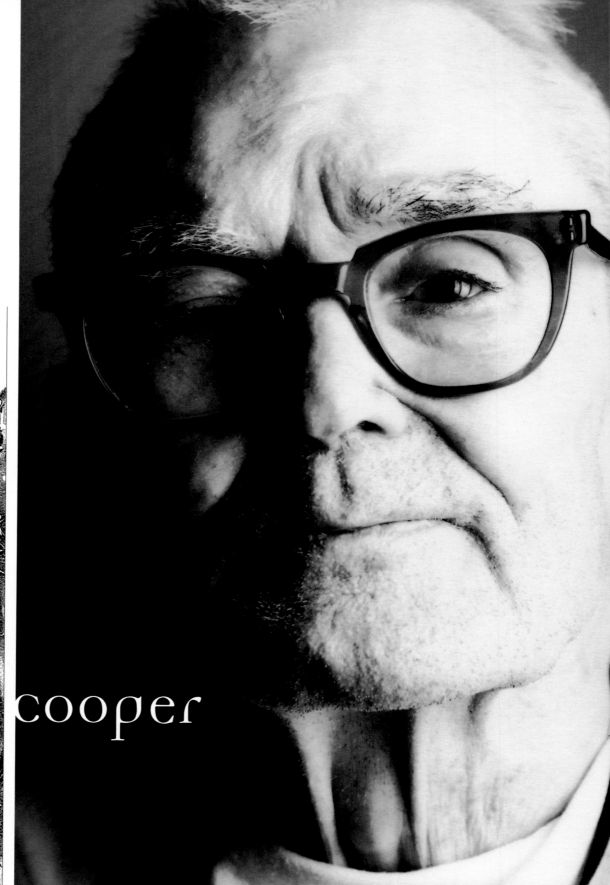

(75

murder grant cooper

organized crime associate

attempted murder

jewel martin (75)

"cut a guy's throat. He tried to
hit me with a metal cake pan."

james (50) brinson
MURDER

"This guy was fitting to kill my nephew, so I challenged him to a shootout."

oh, my gypsy blood got to boiling again. this fellow tried to kill me with a pole ax and i beat him to it and shot him and he died. course, i may have killed him, but i may have not. could have been a heart attack, but, well i can tell you how it was if you want to know. i shot him and he was coming at me and whenever i shot him, he just changed course, running on up a hill towards his house. got up there on the hill and keeled over. but he'd been in the hospital a few times for a heart condition and i don't think i killed him. i think he died of a heart attack. they got me in here all on a big lie. i need a trial for a false arrest. course i shot the man and he died, but they changed it around and made a big assed lie out of it, ya know. and it is lies, not the truth. ya, he come at me. i never done nothing till he come at me, but they don't consider self defence here in alabama. they don't even consider it. i believe that alabama's got the worst laws in the union.

(88) james veach

murder

JOHN McGuire (81)

murder "I had 40 years. I just got over three years left... my people are dead."

murder (68)

Thurmon Jetton

"I feel like I played in hell, is what I feel like."

well, I took up with a man's wife. me and him's been up about it a couple times. He come over one night. I was bad drunk. she was too. me and him got to argue. I brought out the ball bat. she's lying on the bed. And I grab the ball bat to kill him. no use denying that I'm gonna kill him. Just as I swung at him, she run out and run between me and him and caught her right there—killed her deader than a doornail.

I've been making whiskey since I was 14 years old. I been in a federal penitentiary in '68 to '69... then I went to florida, worked down there, stayed down there for seven years. come back here and got in all this mess.

I started to have what they call these seizures. I don't know what they are. you know, when I drink too much whiskey. stayed drunk so long all that whiskey got out at me. That's when I started having those seizures. I've never been to a place yet and stayed more than four or five days without winding up in jail. It's true! I got in virginia one evening and was in jail before 8 o'clock that night for fightin' ■

Dewey **(73)**
Grimes
"I got caught messing
with my gal too young."
sex crime

robert smith (55)

trafficking

"I believe that half
of the population
of the united states
is behind bars."

the problem is, as I see, is that we've got about as much criminals in our leaders as
we do in anything else. I'm not saying that just because the president got into the
shape that he's in, because a lot of them have done just as bad as he is. My biggest
trouble was I wasn't going before the parole board to see what they had to offer me.
see what the parole board had to say about it, instead of the parole officer all the
time. I let the parole officer on my case. he's talking about, "you come up for parole
in the next six or seven months, I'll be the first one to sign it for you to get out." time
to find out he was the one working harder than anybody else to get me back in here ∎

woodrow williams (82) burglary

Leon Joseph Taylor (52)

Habitual offender

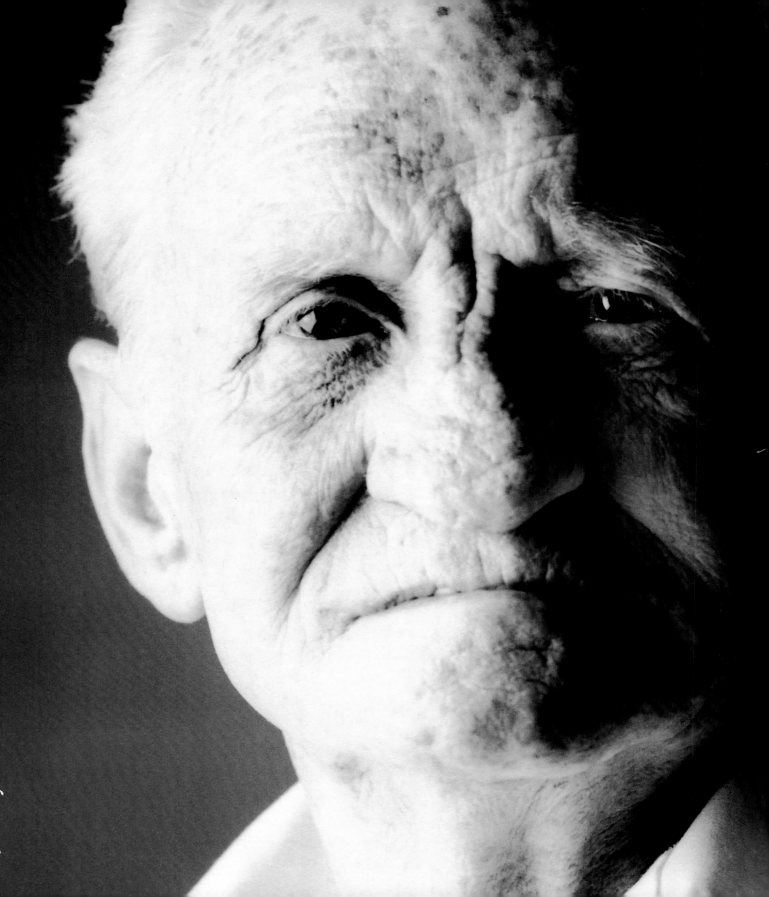

(74) **Ralph works** MURDER

"got eight kids, four boys in a penitentiary."

(79) Robert Johnson

MURDER

KILLED·HIS·ENTIRE·FAMILY.

TESTIMONY OF ROBERT A. JOHNSON

A DISCIPLE IN PRISON

Dear Friends,

Jesus said; "Believe in me." I believe!

I am an inmate in the North Carolina prison system. I have been down since September 8th, 1971.

On December the 6th, 1971 I got on bended knees one night, looking up into the heavens. I asked Jesus to take me as one of His own and forgive me of my terrible sins. He did! He cleaned my heart and made me a new creature.

I begin to serve Him here in prison.

Two and one half years later I begin to write about my experiences of serving Jesus while in prison. In 1975 my book "Disciple in Prison" was published.

God's lovely people all over the U.S.A. began to write to me. I began a newsletter called "Jesus Now" to reach out to all those people.

The returns have been wonderful. God has truly blessed me and given me a near free life here in prison. My heart and mind are free while my body is controlled by the state.

The last week of July 1995 I suffered a congested heart, shortness of breath, and weakness. Jesus sure took care of that. Within three days I was on the surgery table in Durham Hospital getting a triple bypass put into my heart arteries. It was God's dealing with the doctors and people in charge that got me through that critical time.

I praise His holy name! Today at 74 years of age I have no pains. I sleep well because I believe Jesus and I know He cares for me.

Used by permission of DON HOLT (CHRISTIAN TESTIMONIES ONLINE)

Joseph (suits (54)

while avoiding being shot at, he accidentally hit two cars and received a five year sentence for it.

I was dating this lady, and her daughter was strung out on drugs. I was instrumental in getting her finances taken away from her so she could surrender to a rehab and get help from the government. she developed this hatred towards me. so when I went to the house to pick up her mother, the girl answers the door and starts cussing me. I stood there trying to talk to her, but she's crazed, you know, strung out on drugs. so she tells me "if you don't get out of here I'll shoot you, and I'll tell the police you tried to break in on me."

well this girl was out of her mind. I know the house, and I know beside the door there's all kinds of shotguns in there. shoot, that's how I lost my leg. she got me with a shotgun wound and I didn't want another. I've experienced shotgun wounds before.

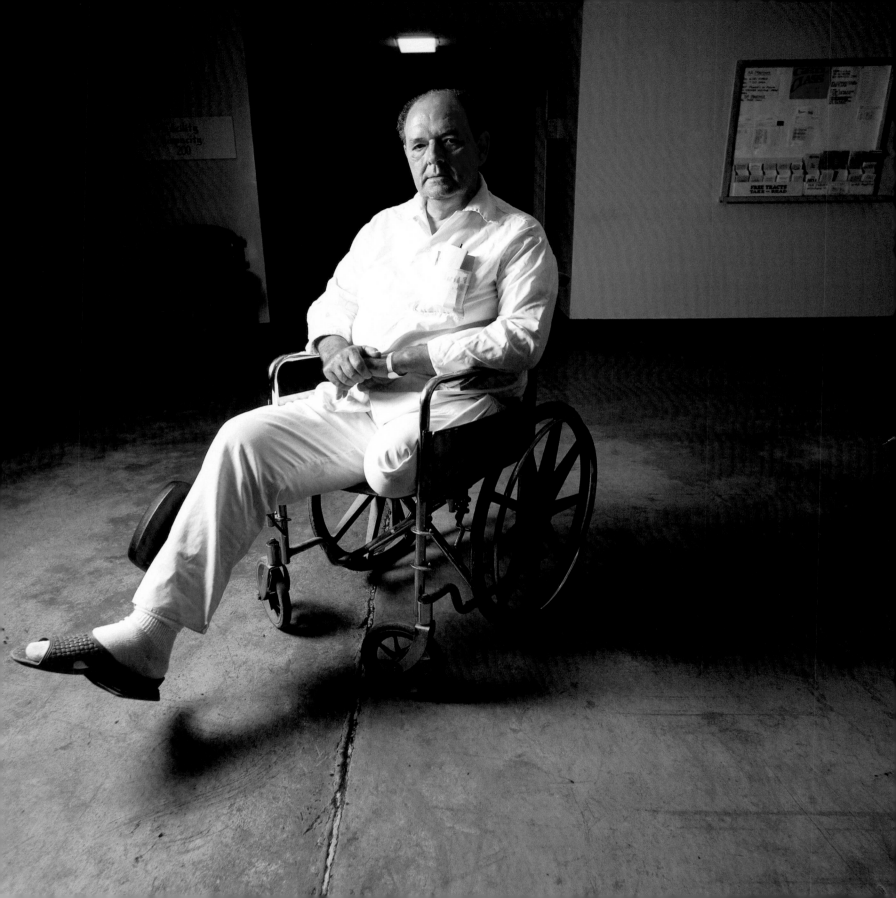

(51) **Jeff**
MURDER
paquette

I shot my wife while I was intoxicated. I don't know why I did it. I was in a blackout. I had no idea why I did it. I was depressed. I'm bipolar. I had gone off of my medication. She was laying dead in the bed. She was still breathing. But it was too late, I guess. I don't remember even calling the police.

I have two artificial hips, I'm bipolar, ulcer-riticulitis, high blood pressure. I've had one aneurysm in my brain. That's why I'm at Warkworth (PRISON). This is considered to be a good facility for medical. And I tell you, you don't want to see a bad one ∎

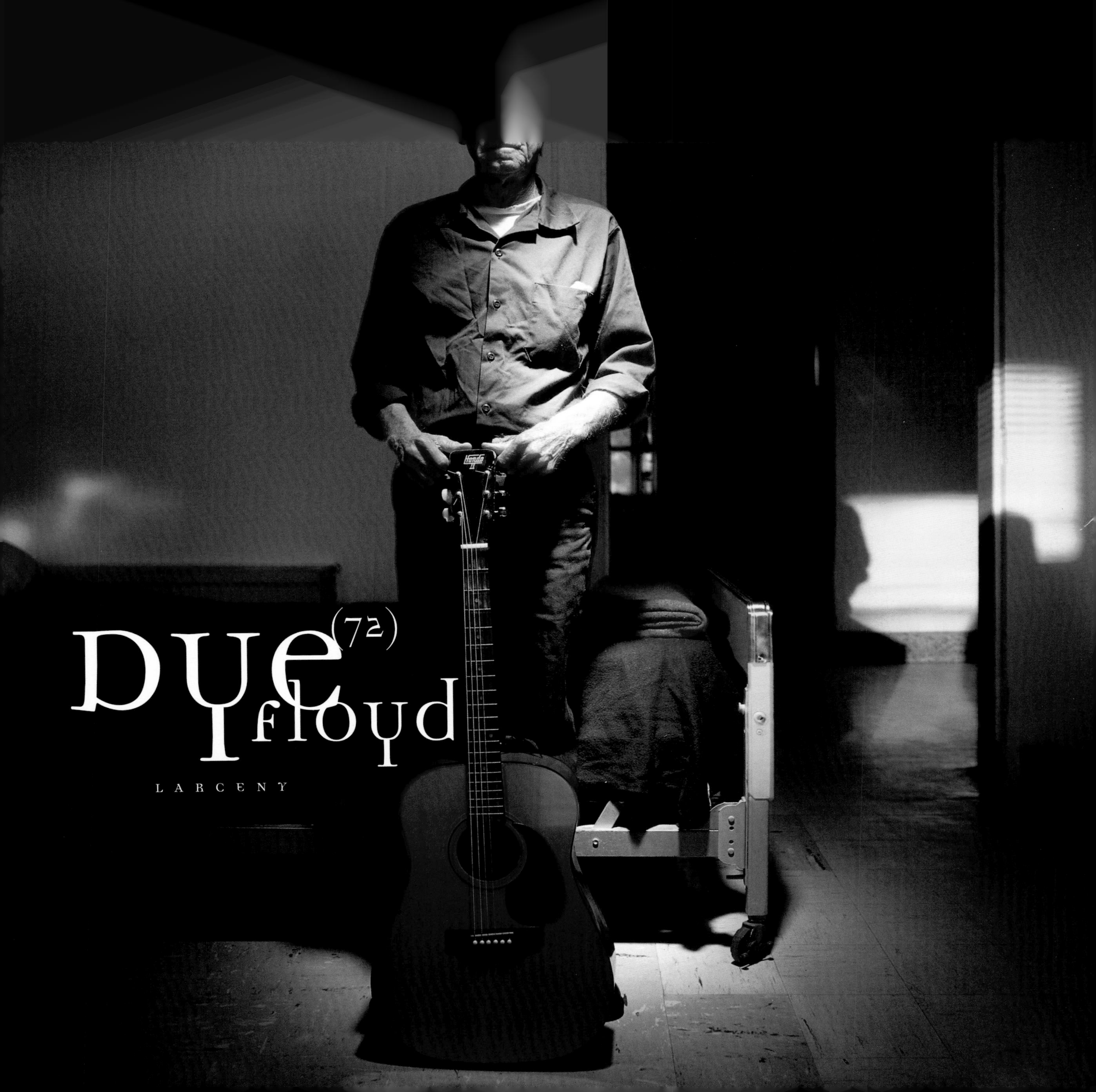
Due (72)
Floyd
LARCENY

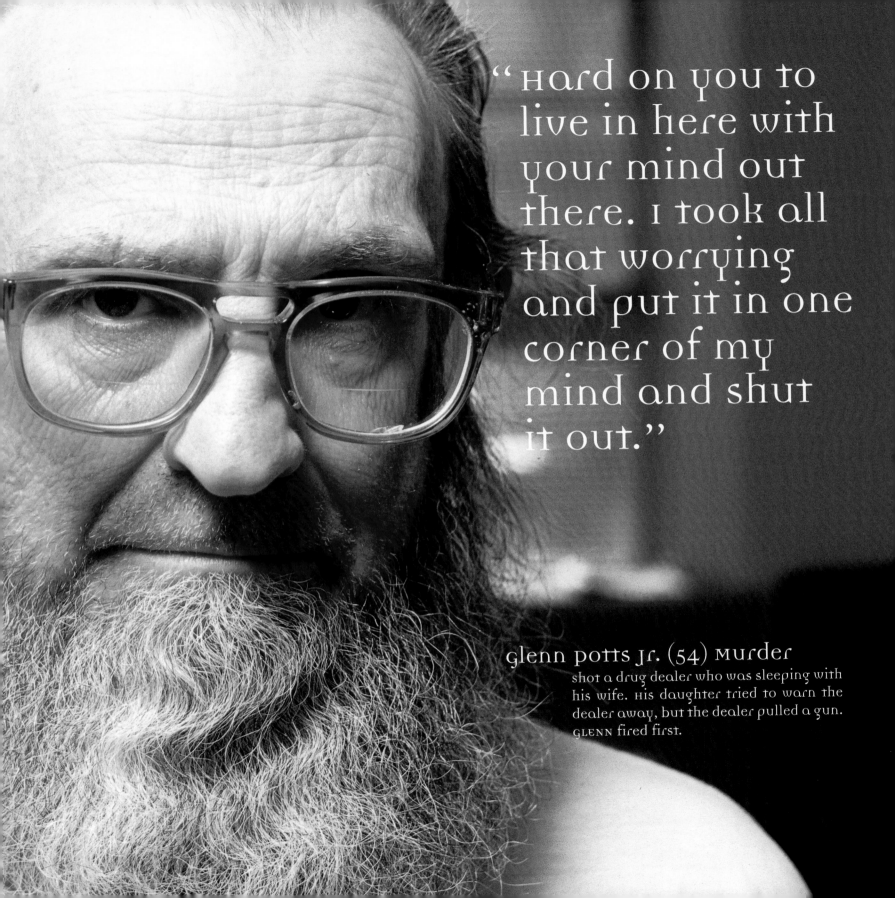

"Hard on you to live in here with your mind out there. I took all that worrying and put it in one corner of my mind and shut it out."

glenn potts jr. (54) murder

shot a drug dealer who was sleeping with his wife. his daughter tried to warn the dealer away, but the dealer pulled a gun. glenn fired first.

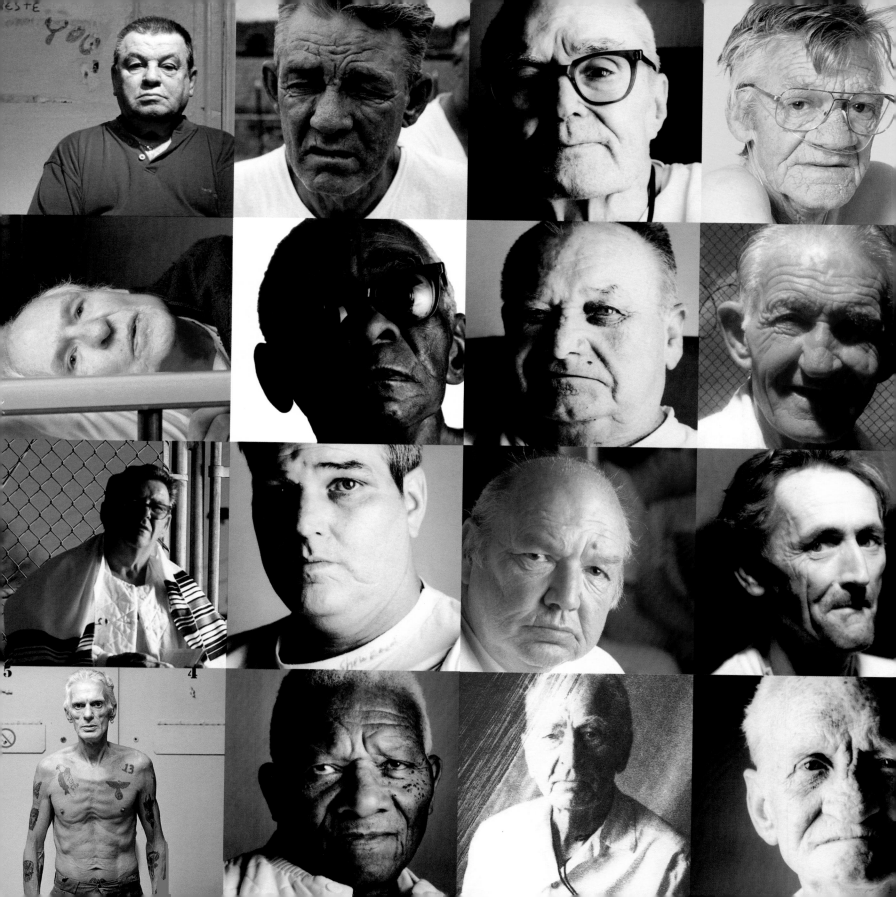

1	2	3	4
5	6	7	8
9	10	11	12
13	14	15	16

(deceased)

The following participants in the "prisoners of age"
book passed away during the term of this project.

1   Marcel Carrière

2   Henry Chandler

3   Grant Cooper

4   Billy Dunn

5   Leo Eason

6   Elliot Gray

7   Dewey Grimes

8   Thurmon Jetton

9   Herschel Kunstek

10 Terry Moore

11 Truman Purdy

12 Rufus Rawls

13 Jules Sauvageau

14 Sam Scott

15 James Veach

16 Ralph Works

our sincere gratitude: to the following sponsors

CONTACT LAB
Montreal, Quebec
514. 523. 2687 Raymond Cantin

KAYJON GRAPHIQUES INC.
Ville St. Laurent, Quebec
514. 333. 1933 Hy Kanner, John James
www.kayjon.com

UNIQUE PHOTO
Florham Park, New Jersey
973. 377. 5555 Customer Service
www.uniquephoto.com

BLACKSTONE WINERY
Graton, California
707. 824. 2585 Sonia Barwick
www.blackstone-winery.com

BAREFOOT CELLARS/GRAPE LINKS, INC.
Santa Rosa, California
800. 750. 8828 Adrienne Barner
www.barefootwine.com

SPRING HILL CHEESE
Petaluma, California
707. 762. 3446 Larry Peter
www.springhillcheese.com

SABATE USA
Napa, California
707. 256. 2830 Eric Mercier
www.sabate.com

QUÉBEC GOVERNMENT HOUSE
New York, New York
212. 397. 0200 Jean Frédéric
www.mri.gouv.qc.ca

CANADIAN CONSULATE TRADE OFFICE
San Francisco, California
415. 834. 3180 Andrew Thompson
www.cdntrade.com

NATIONAL PARKS SERVICE
San Francisco, California

GOLDEN GATE NATIONAL PARK
San Francisco, California

AGENCY ACCESS
New York, New York
212. 279. 9666 Keith Gentile

JBR LA MAISON DU PAPIER
Lachine, Quebec
514. 636. 5006 Diane Zalusky
www.domtar.com

sharon musgrove for her consistent support and coordination skills; sylvia stanshall and george zikos for their transcription of the prisoner interviews; anne monty for her translations of québec inmates interviews, and her transcription and interviewing of alcatraz guards and ex-inmates; kirk mcgregor, ladislaw kadyszewski and marc bider for suffering through weeks of assisting; felicia cohen-rowe for her amazing computer design of the multimedia cd; arlene bradley at foreman ideal; gerry lipnowski for his incomparable editing skills; silvi sills for her meticulous proof reading and co-editing; alison hood for helping us get the whole process off the ground at alcatraz; roland comtois for his tireless research and transcription of the québec inmates interviews; cecilia salado for her design of the website; rachel hawes, and marie reumont for lending an eye; joan melanson at the cbc (canadian broadcasting corporation) in toronto for planting the seed of curiosity; raymond cantin and christine canpan at contact lab for their commitment to the project; hy kanner, john james and lionel fontaine at kayjon graphics for their quality printing work and patience; scott farestad at unique photo for his support and enthusiasm; françois pauzé at kodak canada for taking a chance; diane zalusky at jbr la maison du papier for her expertise; andrew thompson at the canadian consulate trade office in san francisco for his help with the opening; jean frédéric at the québec government house in new york; all the rangers at alcatraz for looking so good under such constant pressure; and noah wou, rebecca manrique, jared lee, andrew tom, and tanner liou for making life so wonderful.

special Thanks

(for stephanie, my wife and partner, whose understanding, love and encouragement made this project a reality. RON LEVINE
to my wife silvi, for her love, vision and inspiration. MICHAEL WOU

Thanks also to Gary Crutchfield, Captain Joe Robertson, Officer Ronald Contrell, Warden Billy Owen, Warden W.C. Berry, Nick Lavrov, Esther Charron, Lisa Mann, Frank Azarch, Celine Laplante, Chris Stafford, Marie-Andrée Drouin, Jonathan Turley, Margaret-Anne Pierre, Lise Madore, Frank Meo, Joan Fraser, Susan Green, Robert Hough, Alain Cloutier, Keith Gentile, Clover Earl, Linda Chalmers, Jim Francis, John Odie, Mona Hakim, Sylvain Campeau, Galerie VU in Québec City, Jenny Green, René Decarufel, Warren Lipton and Margo Lande, Celia Ipiotis, Krista Elkin, Richard Folliguet, Fred and Esther Levine; John and Nancy Wou; Troy Morehouse, Kwi and Oswaldo; Diane, Ian, Robert and Samantha Samberg; Larry and Caroline Levine; Ron, Christine, Christian and Harrison Shewchuk; Loraine Galarneau and Christine Sills; Suzanne and Harry Klein and, as always, Rubicon Grey. We'd also like to thank Corrections Canada, P.O.P.S (THE PROJECT FOR OLDER PRISONERS) of Tulane University in Louisiana, the Alabama Department of Corrections, the North Carolina Department of Corrections; the corrections officers and personnel at the Hamilton Institute for the Aged and Infirm, the McCain Correctional Hospital, Leclerc Institution, Archambault Institution, Ste. Anne-des-Plaines Institution and Warkworth Institution for their support during this project.

ron levine

PHOTOGRAPHER

michael wou

DESIGNER AND CREATIVE DIRECTOR

Ron Levine is an award-winning photographer from Montreal, now based in New York City.

His work has received extensive international acclaim, resulting in exhibits in Colombia, Brazil, Mexico, Poland and Germany, as well as the United States and Canada.

Awards and recognition of Levine's incisive documentary work has come from the Québec Ministry of Culture, Applied Arts Magazine, Canada Council of the Arts and the National Film Board of Canada, among many others. He recently captured The Photo District News "Gold" Award in New York and the CAPIC Grand Prix Award.

In addition, Levine's work has been profiled in a host of publications such as Harper's, Elle, Southern Quarterly, Applied Arts, Hasselblad Forum and Canadian Arts.

He is also a highly sought commercial photographer, and has traveled around the world for a long list of corporate clients.

Michael Wou is the president of Origami Communication Design in Montreal, Canada. He also currently serves as the creative director for New Jersey's Photo Insider magazine. Wou was a senior designer at Gottschalk+Ash International in Montreal and Zurich for several years before founding Origami in 1994.

Wou's many awards include those from How Magazine, Photo District News, and Applied Arts Magazine. His variety of clients range from international corporations to art museums.

He first worked with photographer Ron Levine in 1991, traveling through the American South in search of compelling images and stories. Levine and Wou collaborated again in 1996 to produce an award-winning promotional piece on Florida's alligator wrestling tradition.

Robert "Rosie" Rowbotham

WRITER (FOREWORD)

Rosie Rowbotham is a well-known contributor to a variety of media in Canada, including CBC's national radio show "This Morning." He is also well known for his unconventional background, having served 20 years in prison for cannabis trafficking. He was originally convicted in 1977, and again in 1985, in spite of the support of public figures such as Norman Mailer and Neil Young, among others, who testified on his behalf.

Serving time in the Kingston area penitentiaries of Millhaven and Collins Bay, Rosie acquired a BA in Psychology from nearby Queen's University and a diploma in Business Administration from Seneca College. Rosie became Canadian Managing Director of Prison Life, an award-winning magazine based out of New York.

During his three years with the magazine, Prison Life won prestigious Utne awards. Rosie was also the host and executive producer for a Kingston, Ontario local cable show.

He was released in October 1997, and is currently working on a book of his life.

David Winch

WRITER (INTRODUCTION)

David Winch is an editor and journalist originally from Toronto and currently living in Europe.

As a freelance journalist in Toronto and Montreal throughout 1980's, he covered the film industry, technology, real estate and urban issues for The Globe and Mail, Le Devoir, Cinema Canada, Books in Canada and Montreal Review. He also served as the managing editor of a popular-format national science magazine, as well as copy editor and feature writer for the Montreal Gazette, from 1988 to 1992.

Winch moved to New York City in 1992 to pursue a career as an editor and joined the "Prisoners of Age" project in 1997.

In 1998, Winch moved to Europe, pursuing editorial projects in Ferney-Voltaire, France, near the Swiss border.

Gerry Lipnowski

EDITOR

Gerry Lipnowski, based in Montreal, has been a professional writer and editor for nearly 20 years, working primarily for corporations that are among the largest in Canada. He has won numerous national and international awards for his work in corporate communications, including three Gold Quill awards from the International Association of Business Communicators. Lipnowski has long been an admirer of Ron Levine's photography and has worked with him on a variety of projects prior to "Prisoners of Age."